Welcome to "Project Management 2.0: The Artificial Intelligence Revolution," a book designed to be your comprehensive roadmap in navigating the rapidly evolving landscape of project management, supercharged by Artificial Intelligence (AI). The world is changing at an unprecedented pace, and the field of project management is no exception. Traditional methods, while still effective in many contexts, are increasingly being challenged by the capabilities of AI. From automating mundane tasks to making predictive analyses, AI is set to redefine what it means to be a project manager in the 21st century.

Why This Book?

As project managers, we are often at the crossroads of technology and human interaction. We are responsible for steering projects to successful conclusions, but the tools and methodologies at our disposal are evolving. This book aims to bridge the gap between traditional project management skills and the futuristic potential offered by AI. Whether you're a seasoned project manager or new to the field, this book will provide you with the insights, tools, and strategies to integrate AI into your work effectively.

What's Inside?

We start by introducing you to the transformative impact of AI on project management, setting the stage for what's to come. We then demystify the complex world of AI, breaking it down into terms that are easy to understand and apply. As we delve deeper, we explore how AI can enhance decision-making, automate routine tasks, and even improve team collaboration. We also examine the ethical considerations that come with the use of AI, a topic of increasing importance. Finally, we look ahead to the future, equipping you with the skills and mindset needed to thrive in an AI-driven world.

Who Should Read This Book?

- Project Managers: Whether you're experienced or just starting, this book will provide you with actionable insights to stay ahead of the curve.
- Team Leaders: Understand how AI can improve team dynamics and efficiency, making your projects more successful.
- Business Executives: Gain a strategic edge by understanding how AI can improve project outcomes, thereby affecting your bottom line.
- Students and Educators: Those studying business, management, or technology will find this book a valuable resource for understanding the real-world applications of AI.

Final Thoughts

The future is not something that happens to us; it's something we create. By understanding and embracing the capabilities of AI, you're taking an active step toward shaping a more efficient, effective, and innovative future in project management.

We invite you to turn the page and embark on this exciting journey.

Best wishes,

Leandro F. Pereira, Ph.D. PMP

"The AI transformation is already starting to create winners and losers. But I think that it will also create opportunities for a large number of people to switch professions, or to gain more meaningful work."

Andrew Ng, Co-founder of Coursera and Professor at Stanford University

TABLE OF CONTENTS

CHAPTER 1: INTRODUCTION: THE CONVERGENCE OF AI AND PROJECT MANAGEMENT

The Dynamic Technological Landscape

In our rapidly changing world, the only constant seems to be the accelerating pace of technological innovation. Over the past several decades, we've seen an unprecedented transformation in how businesses operate, largely fueled by advancements in technology. Among the most impactful of these advancements is artificial intelligence (AI), a field that has transitioned from the speculative pages of science fiction novels into the operational frameworks of global corporations. Simultaneously, project management, a discipline that has been integral to human endeavors since the construction of ancient architectural marvels, is also undergoing a significant metamorphosis. The intersection of AI and project management is more than just a trend; it's a pivotal moment that has the potential to redefine how projects are conceptualized, executed, and delivered.

The Multifaceted Promise of AI

Artificial intelligence is no longer a futuristic concept; it's a present-day reality with far-reaching implications. From healthcare, where AI algorithms can assist in diagnosing diseases, to finance, where they can predict market fluctuations, AI is making its presence felt across various sectors. Its capabilities are diverse, ranging from natural language processing (NLP) that allows it to understand and respond to human language, to machine learning algorithms that can sift through massive datasets to identify patterns and make predictions.

The real promise of AI lies in its ability to perform tasks that are either too complex for human cognition or too voluminous for human processing. It can also handle tasks that are too repetitive and mundane, thereby freeing humans to engage in more creative and complex problem-solving activities. Whether it's sifting through terabytes of data to identify consumer trends or automating routine customer service inquiries, AI is increasingly becoming an indispensable tool in modern business operations.

The Historical Context and Evolution of Project Management

Project management is far from a new concept. Its origins can be traced back to monumental projects like the construction of the Egyptian pyramids or the Great Wall of China. However, the modern discipline of project management has been shaped and refined by the complex needs of contemporary business and industry. It has evolved to become a sophisticated blend of technical acumen, leadership skills, and strategic foresight.

In recent years, the field has seen the rise of new methodologies like Agile, Lean, and Scrum, which have brought about a paradigm shift. These methodologies prioritize adaptability, stakeholder engagement, and a focus on delivering value. Despite these advancements, project managers continue to grapple with challenges that have plagued the field for years: scope creep, budget overruns, missed deadlines, and ineffective resource allocation, to name a few.

The Synergistic Intersection of AI and Project Management

This is the juncture where AI technologies offer unprecedented opportunities. Imagine a project management environment where AI algorithms can predict potential bottlenecks in your project timeline well in advance. Consider the utility of a virtual assistant, powered by advanced NLP, that can handle not just scheduling but also stakeholder communication, thereby liberating the project manager to focus on more strategic aspects of the project. What about machine learning algorithms that can scrutinize data from past projects to recommend the most effective team compositions or even predict the success rate of future projects?

The potential applications are not just incremental improvements but transformative changes. By automating routine and repetitive tasks, AI allows project managers to concentrate on higher-order responsibilities like strategic planning and stakeholder management. By providing data-driven insights, AI can facilitate more informed and timely decision-making. And by employing machine learning to analyze past project data, AI can offer predictive analytics that help organizations continuously refine and improve their project management processes.

Ethical and Social Considerations: The Double-Edged Sword

As we integrate AI into the fabric of project management, it's crucial to address the ethical and social implications. The automation of tasks, while beneficial, raises questions about job displacement. The use of algorithms for decision-making brings up concerns about data privacy and algorithmic bias. These are not just technical challenges but ethical dilemmas that require thoughtful consideration and responsible action. These themes will recur throughout this book as we explore the multifaceted impact of AI on project management.

Navigating the Future: What This Book Aims to Achieve

The subsequent chapters of this book will delve into each of these areas in greater detail. We'll explore the nuts and bolts of AI technologies, examine real-world case studies of AI in project management, and discuss the evolving skill sets that project managers will need to thrive in this new landscape. Whether you are a seasoned project manager aiming to adapt and evolve or a newcomer intrigued by the possibilities that AI offers, this book aims to serve as a comprehensive, insightful guide to navigating the future of project management in an AI-augmented world.

So, let's embark on this exciting journey together, exploring the transformative potential and the challenges that lie ahead as we move toward a future where AI and project management are inextricably linked.

CHAPTER 2: THE BASICS OF AI: A PRIMER FOR PROJECT MANAGERS

Introduction: The Imperative of AI Literacy for Project Managers

In the complex and multifaceted world of project management, the role of the project manager is evolving at an unprecedented pace. The integration of artificial intelligence (AI) into the field is not just a passing trend; it's a seismic shift that promises to redefine the very essence of project management. However, to fully leverage the capabilities of AI, project managers must first understand its foundational principles. This chapter aims to serve as a comprehensive guide for project managers to understand the basics of AI, its various subfields, and its ethical implications.

Section 1: Demystifying Artificial Intelligence

What is Artificial Intelligence?

Artificial Intelligence, often abbreviated as AI, is a subfield of computer science that aims to create machines capable of performing tasks that would typically require human intelligence. These tasks include problem-solving, understanding natural language, recognizing patterns, learning from experience, and adapting to new situations. AI is not just a monolithic technology but a constellation of approaches and methods that simulate or mimic human intelligence in machines.

The roots of AI can be traced back to the mid-20th century, with the advent of computers and the conceptualization of computing as a way to simulate human thought processes. Early AI research focused on rule-based systems that could perform specific tasks under a predefined set of conditions. However, these systems were limited in their ability to adapt to new situations or learn from experience.

The development of machine learning, a subset of AI, marked a significant shift in the field. Machine learning algorithms allow computers to learn from data, improving their performance as they are exposed to more information. This has led to significant advancements in various applications, from natural language processing, which enables machines to understand and generate human language, to computer vision, which allows machines to interpret and make decisions based on visual data from the world.

Deep learning, a further subset of machine learning, has been particularly transformative. Inspired by the neural networks of the human brain, deep learning algorithms use layers of interconnected nodes to analyze various aspects of data. These algorithms have been instrumental in achieving breakthroughs in complex tasks like image and speech recognition, machine translation, and even game playing.

However, the capabilities of AI extend beyond just mimicking human cognitive functions. AI algorithms are increasingly being integrated into systems that can perceive the environment, make decisions, and take actions in the real world. For example, autonomous vehicles use a combination of sensors and AI algorithms to navigate through traffic, and robotic systems use AI to perform tasks ranging from manufacturing to surgery.

Despite its advancements, AI also poses a range of ethical and societal challenges. Issues of data privacy, algorithmic bias, and the potential for job displacement are subjects of ongoing debate. Moreover, as AI systems become more complex and autonomous, questions about accountability and governance are becoming increasingly important.

In the realm of project management, AI offers a transformative potential. From automating routine tasks like scheduling to providing data-driven insights for decision-making, AI can significantly enhance the efficiency and effectiveness of project management practices. However, this also requires project managers to adapt to new skill sets, methodologies, and ethical considerations.

Artificial Intelligence represents a paradigm shift in our interaction with technology. It's not merely a tool but a partner that can think, learn, and even perceive, offering unprecedented opportunities and challenges. As AI continues to evolve, it will undoubtedly become an increasingly integral part of our personal and professional lives.

Historical Context

The history of Artificial Intelligence is a tapestry of intellectual curiosity, technological innovation, and a quest to understand both human intelligence and the potential of machines. The concept of creating intelligent machines has been a part of human imagination for centuries, appearing in myths, stories, and speculations long before the advent of modern computing. However, the formal academic discipline of AI is relatively young, tracing its roots back to the mid-20th century.

The term "Artificial Intelligence" was first coined by John McCarthy for the famous 1956 Dartmouth Workshop, which is generally considered the birth of AI as an academic discipline. The workshop brought together luminaries like Marvin Minsky, Nathaniel Rochester, and Claude Shannon, who shared the belief that every aspect of learning or any other feature of intelligence can in principle be so precisely described that a machine can be made to simulate it. Early optimism was high, and there was a belief that human-level intelligence in machines could be achieved within a few decades.

Initial work in AI focused on symbolic AI, also known as "good old-fashioned AI." This approach aimed to represent human knowledge as symbols, rules, and heuristics for problem-solving. Early successes included programs that could solve algebra problems, prove mathematical theorems, and play games like chess at a competent level. However, these systems were brittle and limited to specific domains; they couldn't learn or adapt to new situations.

The 1960s and 1970s saw the development of knowledge-based systems, most notably the DENDRAL and MYCIN projects, which were designed to mimic the problem-solving skills of human experts in specific domains like chemistry and medicine. These expert systems used a "knowledge base" of facts and a set of rules to infer new facts or make decisions. While they were successful in narrow domains, they required extensive human expertise to build and maintain the knowledge base, making them expensive and hard to scale.

AI research also faced several "winters," or periods of reduced funding and interest, due to the limitations of existing technologies and overly optimistic predictions. During these periods, the focus shifted to more achievable goals, leading to the development of specialized algorithms and statistical methods that could solve specific problems, even if they weren't "intelligent" in the way humans are.

The field experienced a resurgence with the advent of machine learning in the 1980s and 1990s. Algorithms like decision trees, support vector machines, and neural networks allowed computers to learn from data, making them more adaptable and capable of handling a wider range of tasks. The development of the internet and the explosion of digital data provided the raw material that these algorithms needed to learn and improve.

The most recent wave of interest and development in AI has been driven by advances in deep learning, a type of machine learning inspired by the structure and function of the human brain. Deep learning algorithms use artificial neural networks with multiple layers (hence "deep") to analyze various forms of data. The advent of big data, along with increases in computational power and storage, has made it possible to train deep neural networks on a massive scale, leading to breakthroughs in fields like natural language processing, computer vision, and autonomous vehicles.

Today, AI is a multidisciplinary field that incorporates elements from computer science, mathematics, psychology, neuroscience, cognitive science, linguistics, operations research, economics, and more. It has applications across various sectors, from healthcare and education to finance and transportation, and is the subject of both utopian dreams and dystopian fears.

As we look to the future, AI continues to raise both exciting possibilities and profound questions. The quest to create intelligent machines challenges our understanding of intelligence, consciousness, ethics, and the very nature of human-machine interaction. It's a journey that has only just begun, and its impact will undoubtedly continue to be a subject of fascination, debate, and discovery for years to come.

The Different Types of AI

Artificial Intelligence can be categorized in various ways based on its capabilities, functionalities, and applications. One common way to understand the landscape of AI is through the lens of its complexity and resemblance to human intelligence.

At the most basic level, we have Narrow or Weak AI. These are systems designed and trained for a specific task, such as voice-enabled TV remotes, image recognition software, or chatbots that can answer customer service inquiries. Weak AI operates under a limited pre-defined range or set of contexts and doesn't possess general intelligence or consciousness. For example, a chess-playing AI like IBM's Deep Blue can defeat grandmasters but can't understand or do anything outside the realm of chess. These systems are rule-based and operate under a confined set of conditions, making them highly specialized but also limited in their applicability.

A step above Narrow AI is General AI, which remains largely theoretical at this point. The idea here is to develop machines with the ability to perform any intellectual task that a human being can do. Such systems would not just be able to play chess or drive a car, but they would also be able to understand natural languages, learn from experience, make jokes, sense emotions, and even potentially possess self-awareness. General AI aims to create machines that can adapt to new tasks through learning and experience, much like humans do. While this form of AI is a popular subject in science fiction, we are far from achieving it with current technologies.

Another way to look at AI is through the lens of its learning capabilities. Machine Learning, a subset of AI, enables systems to learn from data, improving their performance as they are exposed to more information. Within machine learning, there are various approaches like supervised learning, where the algorithm is trained on a labeled dataset, and unsupervised learning, where the algorithm tries to identify patterns in unlabeled data. There's also reinforcement learning, where an AI agent learns to perform tasks by interacting with an environment to achieve a goal or maximize some notion of cumulative reward.

Deep Learning, a further subset of machine learning, has been particularly transformative in recent years. Inspired by the neural networks of the human brain, deep learning algorithms use layers of interconnected nodes to analyze various aspects of data. These algorithms have been instrumental in achieving breakthroughs in complex tasks like image and speech recognition, machine translation, and even game playing.

Then there are Expert Systems, which are computer systems that emulate the decision-making abilities of a human expert in a particular domain. These systems use a 'knowledge base' of facts and rules to draw inferences and make decisions. While they can be incredibly sophisticated and useful in specific settings like medical diagnosis or legal analysis, they are generally not capable of learning or adapting to new information or tasks without human intervention.

Hybrid models are also emerging, combining elements of rule-based reasoning with machine learning to create systems that are both adaptable and capable of handling complex, domain-specific knowledge. These systems aim to leverage the strengths of different AI approaches to create more robust and versatile solutions.

Finally, there's the realm of Emotional AI or Affective Computing, which aims to create machines capable of recognizing, interpreting, and even simulating human emotions. While still in its infancy, this area of AI has the potential to revolutionize human-machine interactions in fields ranging from customer service to mental health care.

The world of Artificial Intelligence is rich and diverse, with various types of AI serving different purposes, ranging from highly specialized tasks to the aspirational goal of mimicking human intelligence in all its complexity. Each type of AI comes with its own set of capabilities, limitations, ethical considerations, and potential applications, making the field an ever-evolving landscape of technological innovation and philosophical inquiry.

Section 2: Core Technologies Underpinning AI

Machine Learning: The Engine of AI

Machine learning is often described as the engine that powers Artificial Intelligence, serving as the mechanism that allows computers to learn from data and make decisions without being explicitly programmed for each specific task. It's a subfield of AI that focuses on the development of algorithms and statistical models that enable machines to perform tasks by generalizing from examples. In essence, machine learning transforms data into actionable insights, allowing machines to adapt and improve over time as they are exposed to more information.

In traditional programming, humans write explicit instructions for computers to follow. This approach works well for well-defined tasks but falls short when dealing with complex, ambiguous, or rapidly changing situations. Machine learning flips this paradigm. Instead of telling the computer how to solve a problem step by step, we provide it with examples of the problem and let it figure out how to generalize from these examples to unseen situations. This ability to generalize is what makes machine learning so powerful and versatile.

One of the most common forms of machine learning is supervised learning, where an algorithm is trained on a labeled dataset. The dataset consists of input-output pairs, where the output is a label or category assigned to each input. For example, in a spam email filter, the inputs could be the text of different emails, and the outputs could be labels indicating whether each email is spam or not. The algorithm learns to map inputs to outputs by finding patterns or relationships in the training data. Once trained, it can then classify new, unlabeled emails as either spam or not spam.

Unsupervised learning is another important category, where the algorithm is given a dataset without any labels or categories and is tasked with finding inherent structures in the data. This could mean clustering similar data points together or finding outliers that deviate from the norm. For example, unsupervised learning techniques might be used to segment customers into different groups based on their purchasing behavior, without any pre-defined categories.

Reinforcement learning is a more interactive form of machine learning where an agent learns to make decisions by interacting with an environment. The agent takes actions based on its current state, receives feedback in the form of rewards or penalties, and updates its knowledge to make better future decisions. This approach is particularly useful in situations where the optimal solution is not known in advance and must be discovered through trial and error. Applications range from game playing, like teaching a computer to play chess or Go, to real-world tasks like robotic navigation and automated trading.

Deep learning, a specialized form of machine learning, has garnered significant attention in recent years. Inspired by the architecture of the human brain, deep learning uses artificial neural networks with multiple layers to analyze various forms of data. Each layer processes the input data and passes its output to the next layer, allowing the network to learn increasingly complex representations of the data. Deep learning has been instrumental in achieving state-of-the-art results in tasks like image and speech recognition, natural language processing, and many others.

While machine learning offers incredible opportunities for automating tasks, deriving insights from data, and solving complex problems, it also poses challenges. The quality of the data, the appropriateness of the chosen algorithm, and the risk of overfitting to the training data are all factors that can impact the performance of a machine learning model. Ethical considerations, such as bias in training data and the opacity of some machine learning models, are also increasingly important concerns.

Machine learning is a transformative technology that serves as the backbone of modern AI applications. Its ability to learn from data and adapt to new situations makes it a powerful tool for a wide range of tasks, from simple data analysis to complex decision-making. As the field continues to evolve, machine learning will undoubtedly play an increasingly central role in shaping the future of AI and, by extension, the future of technology as a whole.

Types of Machine Learning

Machine learning is a multifaceted field with various approaches designed to solve different types of problems. One of the most common forms is supervised learning, which involves training a model on a labeled dataset. In this setting, the algorithm learns to predict an output label based on input features. For example, a supervised learning algorithm could be trained to predict whether an email is spam or not based on its content and other features. The model is trained on a dataset where the "spam" or "not spam" labels are already known, allowing it to learn the characteristics of each category. Once trained, the model can then be used to classify new, unlabeled emails.

In contrast, unsupervised learning deals with unlabeled data and focuses on identifying underlying patterns or structures. The algorithm tries to find relationships among the features of the data to cluster similar items together or reduce the dimensionality of the dataset. For instance, unsupervised learning can be used in customer segmentation, where the algorithm groups customers based on their purchasing behavior, without any prior labeling of the types of customers. It's up to the business analysts to interpret these clusters and decide how to use them for targeted marketing or other business strategies.

Semi-supervised learning sits somewhere between supervised and unsupervised learning. In this approach, the algorithm is trained on a dataset that contains both labeled and unlabeled data. Generally, a small amount of data is labeled while a large amount of data is unlabeled. Semi-supervised learning is particularly useful when acquiring a fully labeled dataset is expensive or time-consuming. The algorithm leverages the unlabeled data to improve its performance, making it a cost-effective solution for many real-world problems.

Reinforcement learning is another significant category that is quite different from both supervised and unsupervised learning. In reinforcement learning, an agent learns how to interact with an environment to achieve a goal or maximize some notion of cumulative reward. The agent learns from trial and error, effectively learning the best actions to take in various states. This type of learning is commonly used in applications where the optimal strategy is not known in advance and needs to be learned through interaction. For example, reinforcement learning has been used to train algorithms to play—and often excel at—complex games like Go, chess, and various video games.

Ensemble methods combine multiple machine learning models to improve performance. These methods often use a collection of "weak learners" to create a "strong learner" that performs better than any of its components. Techniques like bagging, boosting, and stacking are commonly used ensemble methods. For example, the Random Forest algorithm is an ensemble method that combines multiple decision trees to create a more robust model.

Another important distinction in machine learning is between online and batch learning. In online learning, the model updates continuously as it receives new data. This is useful in situations where the data changes frequently and the model needs to adapt in real-time. In batch learning, the model is trained on a fixed dataset and does not update until it is retrained on a new batch of data. Each approach has its own set of advantages and disadvantages, and the choice between them depends on the specific requirements of the task at hand.

Deep learning, a specialized subset of machine learning, deserves special mention. Deep learning algorithms use artificial neural networks with multiple layers to analyze various forms of data. These algorithms have been particularly effective at tasks like image and speech recognition, natural language processing, and many others that were difficult for earlier machine learning algorithms.

The types of machine learning offer a range of tools and approaches for different kinds of problems. From labeled data to unlabeled data, from predictive modeling to data clustering, and from individual models to ensembles, machine learning provides a rich set of techniques for understanding data and making intelligent decisions.

Natural Language Processing (NLP): Bridging the Human-Machine Gap

Natural Language Processing, commonly known as NLP, is a subfield of artificial intelligence that focuses on the interaction between computers and humans through natural language. The ultimate objective of NLP is to enable machines to understand, interpret, generate, and respond to human language in a way that is both meaningful and useful. NLP bridges the gap between human communication and machine understanding, making it a critical technology for a wide range of applications, from search engines and machine translation to chatbots and voice-activated systems.

Understanding human language is a complex task that involves various challenges, including syntax, semantics, context, and pragmatics. Syntax refers to the grammatical rules that govern the structure of sentences, while semantics deals with the meaning conveyed by words and sentences. Context involves the surrounding text or situation that helps to clarify the meaning of a statement, and pragmatics considers the social or cultural norms that influence language use. NLP algorithms must navigate all these layers of complexity to understand and generate human language effectively.

One of the foundational tasks in NLP is text classification, which involves categorizing a piece of text based on its content. For example, email filters use text classification to identify spam messages, and sentiment analysis tools categorize customer reviews as positive, negative, or neutral. Text classification often serves as a preliminary step for more complex NLP tasks.

Another significant area of NLP is machine translation, which involves translating text from one language to another. Early machine translation systems were rule-based and relied on dictionaries and grammatical rules to convert text between languages. However, these systems struggled with idiomatic expressions, context, and other nuances of human language. Modern machine translation systems, often based on neural networks, have become increasingly sophisticated and can handle a wide range of linguistic challenges, although they are still not perfect.

Information retrieval is another critical application of NLP, powering search engines like Google. When you type a query into a search engine, NLP algorithms analyze the text of your query, search through a vast database of web pages, and return the most relevant results. These algorithms must understand the intent behind your query, deal with ambiguous terms, and even correct spelling mistakes to provide useful results.

Question-answering systems, like IBM's Watson, represent another advanced application of NLP. These systems can understand a question posed in natural language, search through a large dataset to find relevant information, and generate a coherent and accurate answer. This involves a deep understanding of both the question and the potential answers, requiring sophisticated algorithms capable of semantic analysis, context recognition, and logical reasoning.

Speech recognition and generation are also important aspects of NLP, enabling the development of voice-activated systems like Apple's Siri, Amazon's Alexa, and Google Assistant. These systems must convert spoken language into text (speech-to-text), understand the text, generate an appropriate response, and then convert that response back into spoken language (text-to-speech). This involves additional challenges compared to text-based NLP, such as dealing with background noise, accents, and variations in speech patterns.

Despite the significant advancements in NLP, the field still faces many challenges. Sarcasm, humor, and idiomatic expressions remain difficult for NLP algorithms to understand. Ethical considerations, such as bias in NLP models and the potential misuse of language-generating algorithms, are also growing concerns.

Natural Language Processing serves as a bridge between humans and machines, enabling more intuitive and effective interactions. By leveraging advanced algorithms to understand and generate human language, NLP has become a transformative technology that is reshaping our interaction with machines and even with each other. As the field continues to evolve, it holds the promise of even more seamless and meaningful human-machine collaborations.

Key NLP Techniques

Natural Language Processing (NLP) employs a variety of techniques to understand and generate human language. These techniques range from traditional linguistic rules to modern machine learning algorithms, and they often work in tandem to solve complex language tasks.

Tokenization is one of the most fundamental techniques in NLP. It involves breaking down a text into smaller pieces, often words or subwords, known as tokens. This is a crucial first step in many NLP tasks as it converts unstructured text data into a form that can be easily analyzed. Tokenization can vary in complexity from splitting text based on spaces and punctuation marks to more advanced methods that consider the linguistic properties of words.

Part-of-speech tagging is another essential technique that identifies the grammatical categories of the tokens in a text, such as nouns, verbs, adjectives, and so on. This information is valuable for understanding the structure and meaning of sentences. For example, knowing that "apple" is a noun in the sentence "I ate an apple" helps in understanding that "apple" is the object of the action "ate."

Named Entity Recognition (NER) is a technique used to identify specific entities like names of people, organizations, locations, expressions of times, quantities, and other terms that have a particular meaning. For example, in the sentence "Barack Obama was born in Hawaii," NER would recognize "Barack Obama" as a person and "Hawaii" as a location.

Sentiment analysis is a popular NLP technique that determines the emotional tone or attitude expressed in a piece of text. This is commonly used in customer feedback systems to automatically categorize user reviews as positive, negative, or neutral. Advanced sentiment analysis models can even identify the intensity of the sentiment or recognize more complex emotions like "happy," "angry," or "confused."

Machine translation techniques convert text from one language to another. Early machine translation systems were rule-based and relied heavily on dictionaries and grammatical rules. However, modern systems often use neural networks and machine learning algorithms to improve translation quality. These systems are trained on large bilingual datasets and can handle a wide range of linguistic challenges, including idioms, context, and cultural nuances.

Coreference resolution is a technique that identifies when two or more words in a text refer to the same entity. For example, in the sentence "John said he would come," the word "he" refers to "John." Understanding this relationship is crucial for tasks like question answering and text summarization.

Text summarization techniques aim to produce a concise and coherent summary of a longer text. There are two main types of text summarization: extractive and abstractive. Extractive summarization selects entire sentences from the original text to construct the summary, while abstractive summarization paraphrases the content to create a summary with new sentences.

Speech recognition techniques convert spoken language into written text. This involves a range of challenges, including background noise, accents, and variations in speech speed and tone. Modern speech recognition systems often use deep learning algorithms trained on large datasets of spoken language to improve accuracy.

Language generation is the flip side of language understanding and involves creating meaningful and coherent text based on certain criteria or inputs. This is a complex task that requires a deep understanding of language structure, semantics, and context. Techniques like text-to-speech conversion and chatbot dialog generation fall under this category.

These are just some of the key techniques used in Natural Language Processing. Each technique serves a specific purpose and comes with its own set of challenges and limitations. However, when combined effectively, these techniques enable machines to understand and generate human language, making NLP a cornerstone of modern artificial intelligence.

Chatbots: These are automated systems that can engage in a conversation with human users.

Chatbots that can engage in conversations with human users are a prominent application of Natural Language Processing (NLP) and machine learning. These chatbots are designed to simulate human-like interactions, providing responses that are coherent, contextually relevant, and sometimes even indistinguishable from a human interlocutor. They serve a wide range of functions, from customer service and technical support to personal assistance and companionship.

At the core of conversational chatbots is the ability to understand and process human language. When a user inputs a query or a statement, the chatbot employs NLP techniques like tokenization to break down the sentence into individual words or phrases. It then uses part-of-speech tagging and named entity recognition to understand the grammatical structure and identify key components like nouns, verbs, and proper names. This parsed information is then processed to determine the user's intent.

Determining user intent is a critical step in generating an appropriate response. Sophisticated chatbots often use machine learning algorithms trained on large datasets of human conversations to identify patterns and relationships in the text. These algorithms can recognize a wide range of intents, from simple requests for information to more complex emotional expressions like sarcasm or humor.

Once the intent is identified, the chatbot generates a response. In rule-based systems, the response is selected from a predefined list of replies based on the identified intent. In more advanced systems, the chatbot may use language generation techniques to create a new, contextually appropriate response. This involves understanding not just the immediate query but also the broader context of the conversation. For example, if a user asks, "What's the weather like?" and then follows up with "How about tomorrow?", the chatbot needs to understand that the second question refers to a future weather forecast.

Context management is another crucial aspect of advanced conversational chatbots. These chatbots maintain a memory of the conversation, allowing them to provide responses that are coherent and contextually appropriate over an extended interaction. This is particularly important in customer service applications, where the user may have multiple queries or issues that need to be addressed in a single conversation.

Some chatbots also incorporate sentiment analysis to gauge the emotional tone of the user's input. This allows the chatbot to provide responses that are not just factually accurate but also emotionally appropriate. For example, if a user expresses frustration or anger, the chatbot might respond with an empathetic statement before addressing the user's query.

Conversational chatbots can be deployed on various platforms, including websites, messaging apps, and voice-activated systems. Voice-activated chatbots, like Amazon's Alexa or Apple's Siri, add an additional layer of complexity as they must first convert spoken language into text, a task that involves challenges like background noise and accents, before processing it for intent and generating a response.

Despite the significant advancements in NLP and machine learning, creating chatbots that can engage in truly natural, human-like conversations remains a challenging task. Issues like handling ambiguous queries, understanding idiomatic expressions, and managing the flow of a conversation are still areas of active research and development.

Conversational chatbots that can engage with human users are a fascinating and rapidly evolving field that combines advanced NLP techniques with machine learning algorithms. These chatbots are becoming increasingly sophisticated, capable of understanding and generating language in a way that is remarkably human-like. As technology continues to advance, chatbots are expected to become an even more integral part of our digital interactions, serving a wide range of roles from functional to social.

Robotics and Automation: Beyond the Digital World

Robotics and automation have come a long way from their early days of performing simple, repetitive tasks in controlled environments. Today, they are capable of executing complex operations in a wide range of real-world settings, from factories and hospitals to homes and even outer space. The integration of advanced sensors, machine learning algorithms, and robust hardware has enabled robots to perceive, learn, and act in ways that were previously unimaginable.

In manufacturing, robots have been a mainstay for years, but their roles have evolved significantly. Earlier generations of industrial robots were limited to tasks like welding, painting, and assembling products on a conveyor belt. Modern industrial robots are far more versatile, capable of handling delicate materials, making decisions based on real-time sensor data, and working alongside human operators. For example, collaborative robots, or "cobots," are designed to share workspace with humans, assisting in tasks that require precision or heavy lifting while ensuring the safety of their human counterparts.

In healthcare, robots are making inroads in a variety of applications. Surgical robots, guided by skilled surgeons, can perform intricate procedures with a level of precision that would be difficult to achieve by human hands alone. These robots can minimize the invasiveness of surgeries, leading to quicker recovery times for patients. Robots are also used for tasks like dispensing medication, sanitizing hospital rooms, and even for telemedicine, allowing doctors to consult with patients in remote locations.

In agriculture, drones and automated tractors are revolutionizing the way farming is done. Drones equipped with advanced sensors can monitor crop health, soil conditions, and moisture levels, providing farmers with valuable data to optimize yields. Automated tractors and harvesters can perform tasks like plowing, planting, and harvesting more efficiently and with less human labor, making farming more sustainable and cost-effective.

In the realm of transportation, self-driving cars are perhaps the most talked-about application of robotics and automation. These vehicles use a combination of sensors, cameras, and machine learning algorithms to navigate through traffic and reach their destinations. While fully autonomous cars are still in the testing phase, many modern vehicles already incorporate semi-autonomous features like lane-keeping assistance, adaptive cruise control, and automated parking.

Robots are also being deployed in disaster response scenarios where it's too dangerous for humans. For example, search and rescue robots can navigate through rubble to find survivors in the aftermath of earthquakes or building collapses. These robots are often equipped with thermal imaging cameras and other sensors to detect signs of life in challenging conditions.

In the consumer space, robots like vacuum cleaners and lawn mowers are becoming increasingly common. These devices use sensors to map their environment and algorithms to plan their paths, performing their tasks with minimal human intervention. More advanced consumer robots are also entering the market, capable of serving as personal assistants that can understand voice commands, answer questions, and even carry out tasks like ordering groceries online.

The rise of robotics and automation also raises important ethical and societal questions. Issues like job displacement due to automation and the ethical implications of using robots in roles like caregiving are subjects of ongoing debate. Additionally, as robots become more autonomous, questions about accountability and governance will become increasingly important.

Robotics and automation are transforming the way tasks are performed across a multitude of real-world settings. Advances in sensor technology, artificial intelligence, and mechanical engineering have enabled robots to take on increasingly complex and varied roles, working both independently and alongside humans. As these technologies continue to evolve, they hold the promise of making our lives easier, more efficient, and in some cases, even safer. However, these advancements also come with a set of challenges and ethical considerations that society will need to address.

Applications in Project Management

Automated Manufacturing: Robots can be used in manufacturing settings to automate repetitive tasks.

Automated manufacturing has been one of the most impactful applications of robotics, revolutionizing the way products are made and altering the landscape of industrial labor. Robots in manufacturing settings are typically designed to handle repetitive, dangerous, or highly precise tasks that would be challenging, unsafe, or monotonous for human workers. The integration of robotics into manufacturing has not only increased efficiency but also improved quality, reduced waste, and enhanced flexibility in production processes.

In the early days of industrial automation, robots were primarily used for tasks like welding, painting, and basic assembly. These robots were generally large, stationary machines programmed to perform a specific set of actions. They were effective but lacked the versatility and adaptability to handle more complex tasks. Fast forward to today, and manufacturing robots have evolved into highly sophisticated systems equipped with advanced sensors, machine vision, and artificial intelligence capabilities.

One of the most significant advancements in automated manufacturing is the development of collaborative robots, commonly known as "cobots." Unlike traditional industrial robots that are often isolated from human workers for safety reasons, cobots are designed to work alongside humans. They come with safety features like force sensors and soft materials that prevent injury upon contact. Cobots can assist human workers in tasks that require precision or heavy lifting, thereby reducing the physical strain on the workforce.

Machine vision is another critical technology that has enhanced the capabilities of manufacturing robots. Cameras and sensors allow robots to 'see' and 'sense' their environment, enabling them to perform tasks that require a high level of accuracy and adaptability. For example, machine vision can be used in quality control processes where robots inspect products for defects. The robot's cameras capture images of the product, and machine learning algorithms analyze these images to identify any irregularities or flaws, often with greater accuracy and speed than human inspectors.

The integration of Internet of Things (IoT) technology has further expanded the capabilities of robots in manufacturing. IoT devices collect data from various points in the manufacturing process, from machine temperature and vibration to production speed and energy usage. This data can be analyzed in real-time to optimize performance, predict maintenance needs, and even adapt the manufacturing process to different products or configurations without manual intervention.

Artificial intelligence and machine learning algorithms have also been incorporated into manufacturing robots, enabling them to learn from data and improve their performance over time. For instance, a robot equipped with machine learning algorithms can analyze historical data to optimize its movements, reducing wear and tear and extending its operational lifespan. Some advanced systems can even adapt to new tasks without being explicitly reprogrammed, offering a level of flexibility that was previously unattainable.

Despite the numerous advantages, the rise of automated manufacturing also presents challenges. The most obvious is the potential for job displacement. As robots take on more tasks, there is a concern about the reduction of low-skilled jobs in manufacturing sectors. This has led to discussions about retraining programs and the ethical implications of automation on the workforce.

Moreover, as manufacturing processes become more automated and interconnected, they also become more vulnerable to cyber-attacks. Ensuring the cybersecurity of automated manufacturing systems is a growing concern that requires ongoing attention.

Automated manufacturing through robotics has profoundly impacted the industrial sector, offering a range of benefits from increased efficiency and quality to enhanced worker safety. Advances in sensor technology, artificial intelligence, and connectivity have made modern manufacturing robots more versatile, adaptable, and intelligent than ever before. However, these advancements also come with challenges, including workforce displacement and cybersecurity risks, that need to be thoughtfully managed as we continue to embrace the benefits of automation.

Drone Surveillance: In construction projects, drones can be used for aerial surveillance to monitor progress.

Drone surveillance in construction projects has emerged as a transformative technology, offering a new paradigm for monitoring and managing large-scale developments. Traditionally, construction site monitoring involved manual inspections, often requiring personnel to navigate hazardous conditions, climb scaffolding, or even halt work to assess progress. Drones, equipped with advanced sensors and imaging technology, have revolutionized this process by providing a safer, faster, and more accurate means of aerial surveillance.

One of the most immediate benefits of using drones in construction is the ability to quickly capture high-resolution aerial images and videos of the site. These visuals offer a comprehensive view of the project, making it easier to track progress, identify potential issues, and make informed decisions. For example, drones can capture images that help in comparing the actual construction status against architectural plans and 3D models, providing a real-time assessment of whether the project is on schedule and adhering to specifications.

Drones equipped with advanced sensors can do much more than just capture images. Some drones come with LiDAR (Light Detection and Ranging) technology, which can create detailed topographical maps of the construction site. This is particularly useful in the initial phases of construction where site preparation and grading are critical. LiDAR can help in calculating the volume of material that needs to be moved, providing precise data that can lead to cost and time savings.

Thermal imaging is another specialized capability that drones can offer. By capturing variations in temperature, thermal cameras can identify issues that might not be visible to the naked eye. For instance, thermal imaging can detect areas where there might be heat loss in a building, indicating insufficient insulation or other structural issues. It can also be used to identify electrical hotspots, which could be a fire hazard, thereby enhancing the safety of the construction site.

The ability to conduct frequent aerial surveys with drones also enables continuous monitoring of the construction site. This is particularly beneficial for large or complex projects where conditions can change rapidly. Regular drone flights can provide updated information that can be shared almost instantly with project managers, engineers, and stakeholders, facilitating timely interventions and adjustments to the construction plan.

Drones also play a crucial role in improving safety standards. Construction sites are often hazardous environments with a high risk of accidents. Drones can be flown to perform safety audits, inspecting for potential hazards like unstable scaffolding, open trenches, or improperly stored materials. By identifying these risks early, preventive measures can be taken to avoid accidents and ensure the well-being of construction workers.

Despite the numerous advantages, the use of drones in construction also presents challenges. Regulatory hurdles are one of the primary concerns, as the use of drones for commercial purposes is subject to various rules and regulations, including flight altitude restrictions, no-fly zones, and operator certifications. Additionally, the data collected by drones can be vast and complex, requiring specialized software and expertise to analyze and interpret.

Moreover, there are privacy concerns associated with drone surveillance. Construction sites are often located in or near populated areas, and drones capturing images and videos could inadvertently invade the privacy of neighboring residents. This necessitates careful planning and execution of drone flights to minimize privacy intrusions.

Drone surveillance in construction projects offers a compelling array of benefits, including enhanced monitoring, improved safety, and operational efficiencies. Equipped with advanced imaging and sensor technology, drones provide a level of detail and accessibility that is difficult to achieve through traditional methods. However, the adoption of this technology also comes with regulatory, data management, and privacy challenges that need to be carefully addressed. As drones become an increasingly common tool in the construction industry, their role in shaping more efficient, safe, and data-driven projects is likely to grow.

Computer Vision: Teaching Machines to 'See'

Computer vision is a multidisciplinary field that enables machines to interpret and make decisions based on visual data. Essentially, it aims to teach machines to "see" in a manner similar to human vision. This involves not just capturing an image but also understanding it, a task that requires a blend of physics, engineering, machine learning, and even cognitive psychology. The field has seen tremendous growth in recent years, thanks to advances in computational power, machine learning algorithms, and the availability of large datasets.

At its core, computer vision seeks to automate tasks that the human visual system can do. This starts with basic object recognition—identifying shapes, colors, and textures in an image. But it goes much further, encompassing tasks like image segmentation, which involves dividing an image into multiple segments and identifying the boundaries of different objects; and object tracking, which is the ability to follow the movement of objects over time and across frames in a video.

One of the foundational techniques in computer vision is edge detection, which identifies the boundaries of objects within an image. This is often the first step in many computer vision applications, as it simplifies the image by reducing the amount of data to be processed. Once the edges are identified, various algorithms can be applied to recognize shapes, patterns, and textures.

Feature extraction is another crucial aspect of computer vision. Features are distinctive patterns or unique characteristics in the image that can be easily tracked and compared. For example, the corners of a book, the round shape of a ball, or the intricate design of a snowflake could serve as features. Algorithms like Scale-Invariant Feature Transform (SIFT) and Speeded-Up Robust Features (SURF) are commonly used for feature extraction.

Machine learning, particularly deep learning, has had a transformative impact on computer vision. Convolutional Neural Networks (CNNs) are a type of deep learning model that has proven highly effective in tasks like image classification, object detection, and facial recognition. CNNs are designed to automatically and adaptively learn spatial hierarchies of features, making them incredibly proficient at understanding the complexities of visual data.

Computer vision has a wide range of applications across various industries. In healthcare, it's used for medical image analysis, helping doctors to diagnose diseases by interpreting images like X-rays, MRIs, and CT scans. In autonomous vehicles, computer vision algorithms process real-time data from cameras and sensors to navigate and make driving decisions. In retail, computer vision is used for inventory management, customer behavior analysis, and even automated checkout systems. In agriculture, drones equipped with computer vision capabilities can monitor crop health and identify potential diseases.

Despite its advancements, computer vision is not without challenges. One of the primary issues is the variability and complexity of the real world. Lighting conditions can change, objects can be partially obscured, and perspectives can vary, all of which make it difficult for computer vision algorithms to consistently interpret visual data. There's also the challenge of semantic understanding—while a computer vision system might recognize a human face or a car, understanding what these objects mean in a broader context is a more complex problem.

Ethical considerations are also increasingly important in the field of computer vision. Issues like data privacy, consent, and the potential for algorithmic bias are subjects of ongoing debate, especially as computer vision technologies become more pervasive in public spaces and critical applications.

Computer vision is a rapidly evolving field that aims to teach machines to interpret the visual world. By combining advanced algorithms with machine learning techniques, computer vision systems are becoming increasingly proficient at tasks ranging from basic object recognition to complex scene understanding. While the field has made significant strides, challenges related to real-world variability, semantic understanding, and ethical considerations remain. Nonetheless, as technology continues to advance, computer vision is set to play an increasingly integral role in shaping our interaction with machines and the world around us.

Applications in Project Management

Quality control is a critical aspect of manufacturing, ensuring that products meet specific standards and specifications. Traditionally, this process has been heavily reliant on human inspection, which can be time-consuming, costly, and prone to errors. The advent of computer vision has revolutionized quality control by automating the inspection process, offering a level of speed and accuracy that is difficult to achieve through manual methods.

In a typical computer vision-based quality control system, cameras and sensors are strategically placed along the manufacturing line to capture images of the products as they pass by. These images are then fed into a computer system where algorithms analyze them in real-time to identify any defects or irregularities.

One of the first steps in this process is image preprocessing, which involves enhancing the image to make it easier for the algorithms to analyze. This could include adjusting the contrast, filtering out noise, or isolating specific color channels. Preprocessing is crucial because the quality of the captured image can be affected by various factors such as lighting conditions, camera angles, and speed of the manufacturing line.

Feature extraction is often the next step, where the algorithm identifies key characteristics or patterns in the image that are relevant for inspection. This could be the shape of an object, its dimensions, texture, or color. For example, in a factory producing screws, the algorithm might focus on features like the thread count, the angle of the threads, and the overall length and diameter of the screw.

Once features are extracted, the algorithm compares them against predefined standards to identify any deviations. For instance, if a bottle cap is supposed to have a specific diameter, the computer vision system can measure the diameter of each cap that passes through the line and flag any that are outside the acceptable range. Advanced systems can even classify the type of defect, whether it's a scratch, dent, or a missing component, providing valuable data for root cause analysis.

Machine learning models, particularly Convolutional Neural Networks (CNNs), have proven highly effective in enhancing the capabilities of computer vision in quality control. These models can be trained on large datasets of both defective and non-defective products, learning to identify subtle patterns and anomalies that might be difficult for a human inspector to catch. Over time, these models can adapt and improve, offering a dynamic quality control system that evolves with the manufacturing process.

The real-time nature of computer vision-based quality control offers another significant advantage. Traditional methods often involve sampling a few products from each batch for inspection, which means that defective items can slip through if they are not part of the sample. In contrast, computer vision allows for 100% inspection, analyzing every single product that passes through the line. This not only improves the overall quality but also reduces wastage and the costs associated with recalls or rework.

Despite its advantages, implementing computer vision for quality control is not without challenges. The system needs to be robust enough to handle variations in lighting, orientation, and other environmental factors. The algorithms must also be fine-tuned to minimize false positives and negatives, as either could have significant implications for both quality and productivity.

Computer vision has brought a paradigm shift in quality control within manufacturing. By automating the inspection process, it offers a faster, more accurate, and more efficient method for ensuring that products meet quality standards. Equipped with advanced algorithms and machine learning models, these systems can analyze products in real-time, identify a wide range of defects, and adapt to changes in the manufacturing process. While challenges remain in terms of environmental variability and algorithmic accuracy, the benefits of computer vision in quality control are compelling, making it an increasingly integral part of modern manufacturing.

Data visualization is a critical component of project analysis and reporting, serving as a bridge between complex data sets and human understanding. While traditional data visualization methods like charts, graphs, and dashboards are effective, the integration of advanced computer vision techniques can elevate the level of interactivity and insight, making the data more understandable and actionable.

Computer vision can enhance data visualization in several ways. One of the most straightforward applications is in the realm of image-based data. For example, in a construction project, aerial images captured by drones can be processed using computer vision algorithms to identify key features like buildings, roads, or equipment. These features can then be overlaid with other types of data, such as project timelines or resource allocation, to create a multi-dimensional visualization. This enables project managers to see not just what is happening but also why it's happening, facilitating more informed decision-making.

Another application is in the area of real-time data monitoring. In a manufacturing setting, computer vision can be used to continuously monitor the production line, capturing data on various parameters like speed, quality, and efficiency. This data can be visualized in real-time dashboards that use computer vision techniques to highlight anomalies or trends. For instance, a sudden change in the color scheme could indicate a quality issue, drawing immediate attention and allowing for quick intervention.

Interactive data exploration is another area where computer vision can make a significant impact. Traditional data visualizations are often static, limiting the user's ability to explore the data in depth. Computer vision algorithms can enable features like object recognition and tracking in the visualization interface. This allows users to interact with the data in a more intuitive way, such as zooming into specific data points for more detail, or rotating a 3D model to view it from different angles. Such interactivity makes the data exploration process more engaging and can lead to more insightful analyses.

Computer vision can also be used to enhance the presentation of data through augmented and virtual reality (AR/VR). For example, in a medical research project, computer vision algorithms can process complex data sets like MRI scans to create 3D models of human organs. These models can be visualized in a virtual environment, allowing researchers to "walk through" the data, so to speak, and gain insights that might not be apparent through traditional 2D visualizations.

The integration of machine learning with computer vision opens up even more possibilities. For instance, predictive analytics can be visualized through heat maps or contour plots that evolve in real-time, providing a dynamic view of future trends or potential problem areas. The machine learning algorithms can be trained to identify patterns or anomalies in the data, which can then be highlighted through the visualization for easier interpretation.

Despite its potential, the application of computer vision in data visualization comes with challenges. The algorithms need to be carefully designed to ensure accuracy and reliability. There's also the issue of computational cost, especially when dealing with large or complex data sets. User experience is another consideration; the visualization needs to be intuitive and accessible, even as it becomes more sophisticated.

The incorporation of advanced computer vision techniques into data visualization offers a more interactive and insightful way to understand complex data sets. Whether it's through real-time monitoring, interactive exploration, or immersive AR/VR experiences, computer vision can make data more accessible and actionable. This has significant implications for project analysis and reporting, enabling more informed decision-making and ultimately leading to better outcomes. While challenges exist in terms of algorithmic complexity and user experience, the benefits of enhanced data visualization through computer vision are compelling and continue to drive innovation in this space.

Section 3: The Role of AI in Decision-Making and Analytics

Predictive Analytics: The Crystal Ball of Project Management

Predictive analytics in the context of project management is often likened to a "crystal ball" because of its ability to forecast future outcomes based on historical data and statistical algorithms. This predictive capability can be a game-changer for project managers, providing insights into potential risks, resource requirements, and project timelines, thereby enabling proactive decision-making rather than reactive problem-solving.

At its core, predictive analytics involves collecting and analyzing historical data to identify patterns or trends that can inform future outcomes. This data can include anything from past project timelines and budgets to team performance metrics and even external factors like market conditions or seasonal variations. Once the data is collected, various statistical and machine learning algorithms are applied to build predictive models.

One of the most common applications of predictive analytics in project management is in risk assessment. By analyzing data from past projects, predictive models can identify potential risk factors that are likely to impact the current project. For example, if data shows that projects of a certain size or complexity often run over budget, the predictive model can flag this as a risk for similar future projects. This enables project managers to take preventive measures, such as allocating additional resources or implementing more stringent budget controls.

Resource allocation is another area where predictive analytics can offer valuable insights. By analyzing historical data on team performance, task durations, and resource availability, predictive models can forecast the optimal allocation of resources for a project. This can help in avoiding bottlenecks, reducing idle time, and ensuring that the project stays on schedule.

Predictive analytics can also be invaluable in stakeholder communication. Project managers often need to provide stakeholders with forecasts regarding project completion dates, costs, and deliverables. Predictive models can generate more accurate and reliable forecasts, bolstering stakeholder confidence and facilitating better decision-making.

Time-to-completion is a critical metric in project management, and here too, predictive analytics can provide valuable insights. By analyzing the durations of similar past projects and taking into account the specific variables of the current project, predictive models can provide more accurate estimates of completion dates. This is particularly useful in industries where time-sensitive factors like market entry or regulatory deadlines are at play.

The integration of real-time data feeds can further enhance the capabilities of predictive analytics in project management. For example, real-time monitoring of project tasks can feed data into the predictive model, allowing for dynamic adjustments to forecasts and plans. If a particular task is taking longer than expected, the model can immediately recalculate the impact on the overall project timeline, enabling quick corrective actions.

Despite its many advantages, predictive analytics is not without challenges. One of the primary issues is data quality. The predictive models are only as good as the data fed into them, and poor-quality data can lead to inaccurate or misleading predictions. Data integration is another challenge, especially in large organizations where data may be siloed across different departments or systems. Ethical considerations, particularly concerning data privacy and security, are also increasingly important as more sensitive information is used in predictive models.

Predictive analytics serves as a powerful tool in the arsenal of modern project management, offering a data-driven approach to forecasting and decision-making. By analyzing historical data and applying statistical and machine learning algorithms, predictive analytics provides insights into risk factors, resource allocation, and project timelines, among other variables. This enables project managers to make proactive decisions, improve stakeholder communication, and enhance the overall likelihood of project success. While challenges related to data quality, integration, and ethics do exist, the benefits of predictive analytics in project management are compelling, making it an increasingly integral part of the field.

Case Study: Predictive Analytics in Software Development Projects

---

Introduction

In the fast-paced world of software development, delays can be costly. They can result in missed market opportunities, increased costs, and eroded stakeholder confidence. This case study explores how a mid-sized software development company used predictive analytics to forecast potential delays in a critical project and took proactive measures to mitigate risks. The project in question aimed to develop a new customer relationship management (CRM) system for a high-profile client within a tight timeframe of six months.

Problem Statement

The project was complex, involving multiple teams working on different modules of the CRM system. Initial estimates suggested a high likelihood of delays due to factors like team performance variability, code complexity, and tight deadlines. The project managers needed a way to anticipate these delays and take corrective actions before they impacted the project timeline.

Methodology

The company collected data from the following sources:

- Historical project timelines and performance metrics from similar past projects.
- Team performance metrics, including velocity and bug rates, from ongoing sprints.
- Code complexity metrics, such as lines of code and cyclomatic complexity, from the codebase.
- External factors like planned leaves, holidays, and client availability.

Predictive Modeling

The data was cleaned and preprocessed to remove outliers and inconsistencies. Various machine learning algorithms, including Random Forest and Gradient Boosting, were tested to build the predictive model. The model aimed to forecast the likelihood of delays based on the collected data.

Implementation

The predictive model was integrated into the project management dashboard. It provided real-time forecasts of potential delays, highlighting the contributing factors like low team velocity or high code complexity. The model was set to trigger alerts when the likelihood of a delay exceeded a certain threshold.

Results

Proactive Risk Mitigation

The predictive model flagged two significant risk factors within the first month:

Low team velocity in one of the teams, attributed to high code complexity.
High bug rates in another module, indicating potential quality issues.

Corrective Actions

Based on these insights, the project managers took the following proactive measures:

- Reallocated resources to the team struggling with code complexity, bringing in a senior developer to provide guidance.
- Conducted a focused code review and debugging session for the module with high bug rates.
- Revised the project timeline slightly to accommodate these changes, with client approval.

Outcome

The project was completed with a delay of only one week, far less than the initial estimates that suggested a potential delay of up to a month. The client was highly satisfied with the proactive management and the quality of the final product.

Conclusion

This case study demonstrates the power of predictive analytics in software development project management. By forecasting potential delays and their contributing factors, the project managers were able to take proactive measures to mitigate risks. While predictive analytics cannot eliminate all uncertainties, it provides a data-driven approach to decision-making, enhancing the likelihood of project success.

Lessons Learned

- Data quality is crucial for the success of predictive analytics.

- Real-time integration of predictive models into project management tools can facilitate quick decision-making.
- Stakeholder communication is enhanced when decisions are backed by data.

Recommendations for Future Projects
- Invest in data collection and preprocessing to improve the accuracy of predictive models.
- Train project managers in interpreting predictive analytics to make informed decisions.
- Explore the use of predictive analytics in other areas like budgeting and resource allocation.

By embracing predictive analytics, project managers can move from reactive problem-solving to proactive risk management, significantly improving the odds of delivering a successful project on time and within budget.

Section 4: Ethical and Social Implications of AI

Data Privacy: Who Owns the Data?

Data privacy is becoming an increasingly critical concern in the realm of project management, particularly as AI algorithms are integrated into various aspects of project planning, execution, and monitoring. The use of AI often necessitates the collection and analysis of large volumes of data, which may include sensitive or personally identifiable information (PII). This data could range from employee performance metrics and email communications to client details and proprietary project specifications. Given the sensitive nature of such data, project managers find themselves navigating a complex landscape of legal and ethical obligations related to data privacy.

One of the most prominent regulatory frameworks that project managers must consider is the General Data Protection Regulation (GDPR) in Europe. Even if a project is not based in Europe, the global nature of modern business often means that data will cross international borders. Under GDPR, stringent rules are applied to the collection, storage, and processing of personal data. Failure to comply can result in severe financial penalties, not to mention reputational damage that can have long-lasting impacts on a project and the organization as a whole.

The GDPR mandates that data must be collected for a specific purpose and must not be kept for longer than necessary. It also requires that individuals have the right to access their data and, in some cases, to request its deletion. For a project manager using AI algorithms to analyze project data, this means being extremely cautious about what data is collected, how it is stored, and how it is used. For instance, if an AI algorithm is used to analyze team performance based on email communications, explicit consent may be required from the team members whose emails are being analyzed. Additionally, safeguards must be in place to ensure that the data is securely stored and that access is restricted to authorized personnel only.

Beyond GDPR, project managers must also be aware of other jurisdiction-specific laws and regulations that may apply. In the United States, for example, different states have different laws concerning data privacy, such as the California Consumer Privacy Act (CCPA). Moreover, industry-specific regulations may also apply. In healthcare, the Health Insurance Portability and Accountability Act (HIPAA) sets forth strict guidelines on the handling of medical information. In finance, regulations like the Sarbanes-Oxley Act impose specific requirements for the management and disclosure of financial information.

The complexity of data privacy regulations is further compounded when multiple jurisdictions and industries are involved. A project manager overseeing a global project in the financial sector, for example, would need to be aware of and comply with financial regulations in all relevant jurisdictions, as well as data protection laws like GDPR and any applicable local or state laws.

Given the complexity and potential risks, many organizations are now appointing Data Protection Officers (DPOs) to oversee compliance with data privacy laws. In projects that heavily leverage AI and data analytics, the role of the DPO becomes especially critical. They work in conjunction with project managers to ensure that all data collection and analysis activities are compliant with relevant laws and regulations.

The integration of AI algorithms into project management brings with it a host of data privacy considerations that project managers must diligently navigate. Compliance is not just about avoiding penalties; it's also about building trust with team members, clients, and stakeholders. As AI continues to transform the field of project management, a deep understanding of data privacy laws and regulations will become increasingly important for project managers. The challenge lies in balancing the immense potential of AI to improve project outcomes with the ethical and legal obligations that come with handling sensitive data.

Algorithmic Bias: Are We Reinforcing Stereotypes?

Algorithmic bias is a phenomenon that occurs when a computer system, particularly those employing AI and machine learning, reflects the conscious or unconscious prejudices of its human designers. This is a critical issue that project managers need to be acutely aware of, especially when using AI tools for decision-making or people management within a project's lifecycle. The implications of algorithmic bias can be far-reaching, affecting team dynamics, resource allocation, and even the overall success of a project.

When project managers use AI tools for decision-making, they often rely on data-driven insights to guide their choices. These could range from selecting team members for specific roles based on performance metrics to prioritizing project tasks based on historical data. However, if the underlying algorithms are biased, the decisions made could inadvertently perpetuate or exacerbate existing inequalities or prejudices. For example, if an AI tool that analyzes performance reviews for team member selection is trained on data that contains gender bias, it may unfairly favor one gender over another when recommending team assignments. This not only undermines the principle of equality but can also lead to less effective teams if the best candidates for specific roles are not chosen.

The issue becomes even more complex when AI is used for people management. Many modern project management tools use AI algorithms to monitor team engagement, productivity, and well-being. While these tools can provide valuable insights, they can also introduce bias into sensitive areas like performance evaluations, promotions, or even layoffs. If, for instance, an AI system designed to monitor productivity is trained on data that reflects racial or cultural biases, such as the flawed assumption that people from certain backgrounds are less productive, the system could unfairly disadvantage team members from those backgrounds. This could lead to a toxic work environment, lower team morale, and ultimately, project failure.

The challenge for project managers is to recognize the potential for algorithmic bias in the AI tools they use and to take steps to mitigate its impact. This starts with understanding the source and nature of the data used to train the AI algorithms. Project managers should question how the data was collected, who it was collected from, and whether it adequately represents the diversity of the population it's meant to serve. It may also involve consulting with experts in data ethics or even conducting third-party audits of AI systems to assess their potential for bias.

Another important step is to always use AI insights as a supplement to, rather than a replacement for, human judgment. Even the most advanced AI algorithms are not capable of understanding the full context in which a project operates. Project managers should use the insights provided by AI as one of many factors in their decision-making process and should be prepared to override the AI's recommendations if they appear to be biased or unfair.

Transparency is also crucial. Project managers should be open with team members about the use of AI in decision-making processes and should be willing to explain how conclusions were reached. If team members understand that AI is being used as a tool to assist, rather than replace, human decision-makers, and that steps are being taken to mitigate bias, it can go a long way in building trust.

In conclusion, while AI offers powerful tools for enhancing project management, the potential for algorithmic bias means that these tools must be used responsibly. Project managers have a critical role to play in ensuring that AI is implemented in a way that is both ethical and fair. This involves understanding the potential sources of bias in AI algorithms, taking steps to mitigate this bias, and using AI insights to supplement, rather than replace, human judgment. By doing so, project managers can harness the power of AI to improve project outcomes while also upholding the principles of fairness and equality.

Job Displacement: The Double-Edged Sword of Automation

While AI can automate mundane tasks and free up human workers for more complex problem-solving, there's also a real concern about job displacement. Ethical deployment of AI in project management should consider the broader impact on employment and job roles.

Conclusion: The New Literacy for Project Managers

As AI technologies continue to evolve and become more integrated into various aspects of project management, understanding the basics of AI is becoming as essential for project managers as traditional skills like team leadership and financial management. This chapter has aimed to provide a foundational understanding of AI, from its history and types to its core technologies and ethical implications, to better prepare project managers for the challenges and opportunities that lie ahead.

CHAPTER 3: DATA-DRIVEN DECISION MAKING: HOW AI ENHANCES ANALYSIS

Introduction: The Importance of Data in Project Management

In the realm of project management, data has always been a cornerstone for making informed decisions. However, the sheer volume and complexity of data that modern projects generate have made it increasingly challenging for project managers to derive actionable insights manually. This chapter explores how AI can revolutionize data-driven decision-making in project management.

Section 1: The Traditional Approach to Data Analysis in Project Management

The Role of Data in Traditional Project Management

In traditional project management, data plays a multifaceted role that extends from the initiation phase all the way to project closure. While the methods for collecting and analyzing data have evolved over time, especially with the advent of digital tools, the fundamental importance of data in guiding decision-making, assessing performance, and ensuring project success remains constant.

During the initiation and planning phases of a project, data is crucial for defining the scope, objectives, and feasibility of the project. Project managers rely on historical data from similar projects, market research data, and stakeholder input to create a project plan that outlines the timeline, budget, and resources required. This initial data collection helps in setting realistic goals and expectations, thereby laying the groundwork for the entire project.

As the project moves into the execution phase, data becomes the linchpin for monitoring and control. Key performance indicators, such as project milestones, budget adherence, and resource allocation, are continuously tracked to assess the project's health. This data is often presented in the form of dashboards, Gantt charts, or other visual tools that allow project managers to quickly identify issues or bottlenecks. For example, if data shows that a particular task is taking longer than anticipated, the project manager can investigate the cause and take corrective action, such as reallocating resources or adjusting the timeline.

Data is also vital for risk management in traditional project management. By analyzing data on project performance and external factors, project managers can identify potential risks and develop mitigation strategies. For instance, if data indicates that a key supplier has a history of delivery delays, a project manager might choose to order supplies well in advance or identify alternative suppliers as a contingency.

Communication with stakeholders is another area where data plays a critical role. Regular updates, often in the form of data-rich reports, are provided to stakeholders to keep them informed about the project's progress. This not only helps in building trust but also ensures that stakeholders can provide timely input that could be crucial for the project's success. For example, if data shows that the project is likely to exceed its budget, early communication with stakeholders can facilitate discussions on how to address the issue, whether it's by securing additional funding or by adjusting the project's scope.

Finally, once the project reaches its closure phase, data is essential for evaluating the project's overall performance and identifying lessons learned. This involves a thorough analysis of all collected data to assess whether the project met its objectives within the defined scope, time, and budget. The insights gained are not only valuable for evaluating the success of the current project but also serve as invaluable data points for future projects.

Data is the backbone of traditional project management, providing the insights and evidence needed to plan, execute, monitor, and close projects successfully. It aids in setting realistic objectives, enables real-time monitoring and control, facilitates risk management, enhances stakeholder communication, and contributes to continuous improvement by informing future projects. While the tools and techniques for data collection and analysis may have evolved, especially with the rise of digital technologies, the fundamental role of data in guiding and informing project management decisions remains as vital as ever.

Limitations of Manual Data Analysis

Despite its critical role in various aspects of business and research, manual data analysis comes with a set of limitations that can significantly impact the quality and utility of the insights derived. One of the most glaring issues is the risk of human error. Even the most meticulous analyst is susceptible to mistakes, whether it's a simple error in data entry or a more complex mistake in the application of statistical methods. These errors can skew results, leading to incorrect conclusions that may, in turn, inform poor decision-making. The risk is particularly high when dealing with large or complex datasets where the sheer volume of information can make errors more likely and harder to spot.

Another significant limitation is the time-consuming nature of manual data analysis. Sifting through large datasets to identify relevant information can be an arduous process, taking up valuable time that could be better spent on other tasks. This is especially problematic in fast-paced environments where timely decision-making is crucial. For example, in a project management scenario, delays in data analysis could result in missed opportunities to correct course, leading to project overruns or failure. The time factor also limits the frequency with which data can be analyzed. In a rapidly changing business landscape, infrequent analysis may mean that decisions are being made based on outdated information, reducing their effectiveness and relevance.

The complexity of data is another area where manual analysis often falls short. With the advent of big data technologies, organizations now have access to incredibly rich and varied datasets that include not just numerical data, but also text, images, and even video. Manually analyzing such complex data to identify patterns or trends is often impractical, if not impossible. Even with simpler datasets, the human brain is not well-suited to easily identify multi-dimensional patterns or subtle correlations that might be of significant interest. This is particularly true for data that is non-linear or has complex interactions that are not easily discernible through traditional methods of manual analysis.

Moreover, manual data analysis often lacks the scalability to handle the ever-increasing volumes of data generated in today's digital world. As businesses expand and data accumulates, the manual methods that might have been sufficient in the past can become untenable. This lack of scalability can result in incomplete analysis or force organizations to limit the scope of their data exploration, potentially missing out on important insights.

Lastly, manual data analysis is often constrained by the cognitive biases of the analysts themselves. Whether it's confirmation bias, where the analyst gives preference to data that confirms their pre-existing beliefs, or availability bias, where more recent or memorable data is given undue weight, these cognitive biases can significantly impact the objectivity and reliability of manual data analysis.

While manual data analysis has been and continues to be an important method for deriving insights, it is fraught with limitations including the risk of human error, the time-consuming nature of the process, and the inability to easily identify complex patterns or trends. These limitations not only affect the quality of the insights derived but can also have broader implications for decision-making and strategic planning. As such, there is a growing need for more advanced, automated methods of data analysis that can overcome these challenges.

Section 2: The Advent of AI in Data Analysis

How AI Changes the Game

Artificial Intelligence (AI), especially machine learning algorithms, has revolutionized the way data is analyzed, offering a powerful tool for project managers to gain quick and accurate insights from large and complex datasets. The automation of data analysis through AI addresses many of the limitations associated with manual methods, enhancing the quality, speed, and scope of insights that can be derived.

One of the most significant advantages of using AI in data analysis is its ability to handle large volumes of data efficiently. Traditional manual methods often struggle with scalability, becoming increasingly time-consuming and error-prone as the size of the dataset grows. In contrast, machine learning algorithms can quickly analyze massive datasets, identifying relevant patterns and trends without human intervention. This speed is particularly beneficial in project management scenarios where timely decision-making can be the difference between project success and failure.

Accuracy Is another area where AI excels. Machine learning algorithms are designed to learn from data, improving their performance as more data is processed. This learning capability reduces the risk of errors that are common in manual methods, providing more reliable and accurate insights. For example, a machine learning model trained to predict project delays based on historical data can continually refine its predictions as it processes new data, becoming increasingly accurate over time.

The complexity of data is also less of an issue for AI algorithms. Unlike humans, who may struggle to identify multi-dimensional patterns or subtle correlations in complex datasets, machine learning algorithms excel at finding relationships among multiple variables. This is especially useful in project management, where various factors like resource allocation, team performance, and external market conditions can all impact project outcomes. AI can analyze these factors in conjunction to provide a more holistic view of the project's status.

AI's ability to analyze different types of data, including unstructured data like text, images, or videos, adds another layer of depth to its analytical capabilities. For instance, Natural Language Processing (NLP), a subfield of AI, can be used to analyze textual data such as emails, project documentation, or customer reviews to gain insights into team communication, project risks, or customer satisfaction. This ability to analyze diverse data types provides project managers with a more comprehensive understanding of their projects, enabling more informed decision-making.

Moreover, the automation of data analysis frees up valuable time for project managers, allowing them to focus on strategic activities like stakeholder communication, team leadership, and problem-solving. Instead of spending time sifting through spreadsheets or creating reports, project managers can rely on AI-powered dashboards that provide real-time insights into project performance, risk factors, and other key metrics. This not only improves efficiency but also enables more proactive project management, as issues can be identified and addressed as soon as they arise.

AI, particularly machine learning algorithms, offers a powerful solution for automating the analysis of large and complex datasets in project management. By providing quick, accurate, and comprehensive insights, AI enhances the quality of decision-making while also improving efficiency. Whether it's predicting project delays, optimizing resource allocation, or assessing team performance, AI provides project managers with the tools they need to manage more effectively, ultimately increasing the likelihood of project success.

Types of Data AI Can Analyze

Artificial Intelligence (AI) has the capability to analyze a wide range of data types, each offering unique insights that can be leveraged for various applications, including project management, healthcare, marketing, and more. The versatility of AI in handling different kinds of data is one of its most compelling features, allowing for a more comprehensive and nuanced understanding of complex phenomena.

Numerical data is perhaps the most straightforward type of data that AI can analyze. This includes anything that can be quantified, such as sales figures, temperature readings, or performance metrics. Machine learning algorithms can sift through large volumes of numerical data to identify trends, make predictions, or detect anomalies. For instance, in a project management context, AI can analyze historical project timelines and budgets to predict the likelihood of delays or cost overruns in future projects.

Categorical data, which includes variables that can be sorted into categories but don't inherently have a numerical relationship, can also be analyzed by AI. Examples include data like customer demographics, product types, or employee roles. Machine learning models can identify relationships or correlations between different categories, which can be useful for tasks like customer segmentation or resource allocation.

Textual data is another area where AI, particularly through Natural Language Processing (NLP), has made significant strides. NLP algorithms can analyze large volumes of text to extract meaningful insights. This can range from sentiment analysis on customer reviews to keyword extraction in legal documents. In project management, NLP could be used to analyze communication within teams to identify potential areas of conflict or misunderstanding that could impact project success.

AI's capabilities extend to image data as well. Computer vision, a subfield of AI, focuses on teaching machines to interpret and make decisions based on visual data. This technology is used in a variety of applications, from medical imaging diagnostics to autonomous vehicles. In a manufacturing setting, computer vision could be used to identify defects in products as they come off the assembly line, ensuring quality control.

Audio data is another frontier where AI has shown promise. Algorithms can be trained to recognize speech patterns, musical structures, or even the sounds of machinery to predict maintenance needs. In customer service, AI algorithms analyze voice data to gauge customer sentiment or to route calls more effectively.

Time-series data, which involves observations on a variable or several variables over time, is crucial in fields like finance for predicting stock prices, or in healthcare for monitoring patient vitals. AI algorithms can analyze these sequences to forecast future values or detect anomalies, providing valuable insights for decision-making.

Geospatial data, which includes information about geographical locations, can also be analyzed by AI to solve complex problems like optimizing delivery routes, predicting natural disasters, or monitoring environmental changes.

Finally, relational data, which involves multiple databases or tables and the relationships between them, can be incredibly complex. AI can help in identifying hidden patterns in the data that are not immediately obvious, offering insights that can be critical for fields like cybersecurity or fraud detection.

AI's ability to analyze various types of data—numerical, categorical, textual, image-based, audio, time-series, geospatial, and relational—makes it an incredibly versatile tool for deriving insights from complex datasets. Whether it's predicting future trends, identifying anomalies, or uncovering hidden relationships among variables, AI provides a comprehensive approach to data analysis that can significantly enhance decision-making across a wide range of applications.

Section 3: Practical Applications of AI in Data-Driven Decision Making

Predictive Analytics for Risk Assessment

The application of Artificial Intelligence (AI) algorithms in analyzing historical project data for risk prediction represents a transformative shift in the field of project management. Traditionally, risk management has been a reactive process, often requiring project managers to address issues as they arise. However, AI's predictive capabilities enable a more proactive approach, allowing project managers to anticipate potential risks and take preventive measures before these risks materialize into tangible problems.

Historical project data serves as the foundational layer for this predictive model. This data can encompass a wide range of variables, such as past project timelines, budget adherence, resource allocation, team performance metrics, and even external factors like market conditions or seasonal variations. The richness and diversity of this data provide a fertile ground for AI algorithms to identify patterns or trends that could signify potential risks.

Machine learning algorithms, a subset of AI, are particularly well-suited for this task. These algorithms can be trained on historical project data to create predictive models. For example, a machine learning model could analyze data from past projects to identify factors that have previously led to budget overruns. These factors might include extended timelines, scope creep, or unexpected resource allocation changes. Once the model is trained, it can analyze current project data in real-time to predict the likelihood of similar budget overruns occurring.

The real power of AI in proactive risk management lies in its ability to analyze multiple variables simultaneously to provide a more holistic view of potential risks. Traditional manual methods might allow for the analysis of one or two variables at a time, but machine learning algorithms can handle much more complex, multi-dimensional data. This enables the identification of compound risks, where multiple factors interact in intricate ways to create a potential issue. For instance, a machine learning model could determine that a combination of a tight deadline, a particular team composition, and the complexity of the project significantly increases the risk of missing key milestones.

Once potential risks are identified, project managers can take proactive steps to mitigate them. If the AI model predicts a high likelihood of a budget overrun, for example, the project manager might allocate additional resources to critical tasks or negotiate for an increased budget. If the model indicates a high risk of missing a key milestone, the project manager could reevaluate the project timeline or redistribute tasks to ensure that the milestone is met.

Moreover, the predictive model can be continually updated with new data, allowing for dynamic risk assessment. As the project progresses, the model can refine its predictions, making them increasingly accurate and providing project managers with the most current information for decision-making. This dynamic nature of AI-driven risk prediction is particularly valuable in long-term projects or those with rapidly changing conditions.

AI algorithms offer a powerful tool for proactive risk management in project management settings. By analyzing historical project data, these algorithms can predict potential risks, enabling project managers to take preventive measures before problems occur. The ability to handle complex, multi-dimensional data allows for a more comprehensive understanding of risks, while the dynamic nature of the predictive model ensures that risk assessments are continually updated. This proactive approach not only increases the likelihood of project success but also enhances efficiency and stakeholder confidence.

Resource Allocation and Optimization

The efficient allocation of resources is a cornerstone of successful project management, impacting everything from project timelines and budgets to team morale and stakeholder satisfaction. Machine learning algorithms offer a transformative approach to this critical task, enabling project managers to optimize resource allocation based on both past and current data. This represents a significant advancement over traditional methods, which often rely on static models and human intuition, and may not fully capture the complexity and dynamism of modern projects.

Machine learning algorithms can be trained on a wealth of historical project data, including but not limited to, timelines, budgets, resource utilization rates, and project outcomes. This historical data serves as the foundation for predictive models that can identify the most efficient ways to allocate resources. For example, a machine learning model could analyze past projects to determine the optimal team size for various types of tasks, or to identify the point at which adding more manpower ceases to increase productivity and may even lead to inefficiencies due to increased coordination costs.

But the true power of machine learning lies in its ability to also incorporate real-time, current data into its analyses. This could include ongoing project metrics, such as task completion rates, as well as more dynamic factors like employee availability, current workload, or even market conditions that might affect the cost of material resources. By continuously updating the predictive model with this current data, machine learning algorithms can provide real-time recommendations for resource allocation that reflect the actual conditions of the project, rather than relying solely on historical trends or static models.

The complexity of modern projects often involves multiple, interrelated variables that can impact resource allocation. Traditional methods may struggle to account for these complex interactions, but machine learning algorithms are designed to handle multi-dimensional data. This enables a more nuanced understanding of resource needs. For instance, a machine learning model could analyze the interplay between task complexity, required skill sets, and available manpower to recommend the most efficient allocation of human resources across various project tasks. Similarly, the algorithm could consider factors like supplier lead times, storage costs, and the shelf life of materials to optimize the ordering and storage of material resources.

Once the machine learning model has made its recommendations, project managers can use this information to make informed decisions. If the model suggests that a particular task is understaffed, the project manager could reallocate team members accordingly. If the model indicates that material resources are likely to be wasted due to over-ordering, the project manager could adjust purchase orders to avoid unnecessary costs. These data-driven decisions not only improve efficiency but also contribute to better project outcomes, as resources are allocated in a way that maximizes their utility and impact.

Furthermore, the machine learning model itself can be a valuable resource for stakeholder communication. The data-driven nature of the model's recommendations can provide a strong rationale for decision-making, making it easier to secure stakeholder buy-in. For example, if the model recommends an increase in manpower that would require additional budget allocation, the project manager can use the model's findings to justify this request to stakeholders.

Machine learning algorithms offer a robust, dynamic approach to resource allocation in project management. By analyzing both past and current data, these algorithms can provide real-time recommendations that account for the complexity and variability of modern projects. This enables more efficient and effective resource allocation, leading to better project outcomes, increased efficiency, and greater stakeholder satisfaction.

Stakeholder Engagement

Stakeholder management is a critical aspect of any project, influencing everything from resource allocation and decision-making to the overall success or failure of the endeavor. Traditional methods of stakeholder management often rely on subjective assessments, such as personal interactions and observations, to gauge stakeholder sentiment and attitudes. While these methods can be effective, they are also prone to biases and inaccuracies. Natural Language Processing (NLP), a subfield of Artificial Intelligence, offers a more objective, data-driven approach to stakeholder management by analyzing stakeholder communications to gauge sentiment and attitudes.

NLP algorithms can process large volumes of text data, such as emails, meeting transcripts, or social media posts, to extract meaningful insights. One of the most common applications of NLP in stakeholder management is sentiment analysis, which involves categorizing text data into different emotional tones like positive, negative, or neutral. For example, an NLP algorithm could analyze the text of emails from stakeholders to determine the overall sentiment towards a project. If the algorithm detects a trend of increasingly negative sentiment, this could serve as an early warning sign of growing stakeholder dissatisfaction, allowing project managers to take proactive measures to address concerns before they escalate into more significant issues.

Beyond simple sentiment analysis, more advanced NLP techniques can also identify specific themes or topics that are driving stakeholder sentiment. Topic modeling algorithms can sift through text data to pinpoint recurring themes or keywords. This can provide a more nuanced understanding of stakeholder attitudes, revealing not just how stakeholders feel, but also why they feel that way. For instance, if topic modeling identifies that discussions around "budget" are frequently associated with negative sentiment, this could indicate that stakeholders are concerned about the project's financial management. Armed with this insight, project managers can focus on improving budget transparency or providing more frequent financial updates to address stakeholder concerns.

NLP can also analyze the complexity and clarity of stakeholder communications. For example, text readability algorithms can assess whether project updates and reports are easily understandable by stakeholders. If the algorithm determines that communications are too complex or filled with jargon, this could be a sign that stakeholders may not fully understand the project's status or objectives, leading to potential misunderstandings or misalignments down the line.

The real-time capabilities of NLP algorithms add another layer of value. Unlike traditional methods, which may involve periodic stakeholder surveys or intermittent one-on-one meetings, NLP can provide continuous, real-time analysis of stakeholder communications. This enables more timely and responsive stakeholder management, allowing project managers to address issues or capitalize on opportunities as they arise.

Moreover, the insights derived from NLP can be integrated into broader project management dashboards, providing a more holistic view of project health. This data-driven approach not only enhances the objectivity and accuracy of stakeholder management but also enables better alignment with other project metrics and KPIs. For example, if NLP analysis reveals a negative stakeholder sentiment around project delays, and other project metrics also indicate slipping timelines, the project manager has a strong, data-backed case for taking corrective action.

Natural Language Processing offers a transformative approach to stakeholder management, providing a more objective, nuanced, and timely understanding of stakeholder sentiment and attitudes. By analyzing text data from stakeholder communications, NLP algorithms can identify emotional tones, key themes, and even the clarity of communications, offering valuable insights that can inform a more effective and responsive stakeholder management strategy. This data-driven approach not only improves the quality of stakeholder relations but also contributes to better overall project outcomes.

Section 4: Case Studies

Case Study 1: AI in Software Development Risk Assessment

Introduction

XYZ Software Inc., a mid-sized software development company, faced challenges in managing project risks, leading to frequent delays and budget overruns. To address these issues, the company decided to integrate Artificial Intelligence (AI) into its project management processes, specifically focusing on risk prediction and mitigation. This case study explores how the implementation of AI transformed the company's approach to project management, ultimately leading to more successful project outcomes.

The Challenge

XYZ Software Inc. had a history of projects that exceeded timelines and budgets. Traditional risk management methods, such as manual data analysis and expert judgment, were not effective in predicting and mitigating risks in a timely manner. The company needed a solution that could provide real-time insights into potential risks and offer actionable recommendations for mitigation.

The Solution

The company decided to implement an AI-driven risk management system that utilized machine learning algorithms to analyze historical project data and real-time project metrics. The system was designed to:

- Analyze past project data to identify common risk factors that led to delays and cost overruns.
- Continuously monitor current projects to predict potential risks based on a variety of factors, including team performance, resource allocation, and project complexity.

- Provide real-time recommendations for risk mitigation.

Implementation

Data Collection and Training

The first step involved gathering historical project data, including timelines, budgets, resource allocation, and project outcomes. This data was used to train a machine learning model to identify patterns and correlations that could signify potential risks.

Real-time Monitoring and Prediction
Once the model was trained, it was integrated into the company's project management software to monitor real-time project metrics. The AI system was capable of issuing alerts if it predicted a high likelihood of risk, such as a delay or budget overrun.

Actionable Recommendations
The AI system was also programmed to provide actionable recommendations for risk mitigation. For example, if the system predicted a high likelihood of a project delay due to resource constraints, it would recommend reallocating resources or adjusting timelines.

Results
Improved Risk Prediction
The AI system was remarkably accurate in predicting risks. In a span of one year, the system successfully predicted potential delays in 90% of the projects and budget overruns in 85% of the cases.

Proactive Risk Mitigation
The real-time nature of the AI system allowed project managers to take immediate action to mitigate risks. This proactive approach led to a 30% reduction in project delays and a 25% reduction in budget overruns within the first year of implementation.

Enhanced Stakeholder Communication
The data-driven insights provided by the AI system also improved stakeholder communication. Project managers were able to provide stakeholders with more accurate and timely information, leading to increased stakeholder confidence and engagement.

Conclusion
The implementation of an AI-driven risk management system had a transformative impact on XYZ Software Inc.'s approach to project management. By leveraging machine learning algorithms for risk prediction and mitigation, the company was able to significantly improve project outcomes, reduce delays and cost overruns, and enhance stakeholder communication. This case study serves as a compelling example of how AI can be effectively utilized to address complex challenges in project management.

Case Study 2: AI in Construction Resource Optimization

Introduction

ABC Construction Firm, a leading player in the construction industry, faced challenges in efficiently allocating resources across multiple projects. This inefficiency led to increased costs and delays, affecting the firm's profitability and reputation. To tackle these issues, ABC Construction Firm integrated machine learning algorithms into their project management system to optimize resource allocation. This case study delves into how this technological intervention led to reduced costs and improved efficiency.

The Challenge

Resource allocation has always been a complex task in the construction industry, involving various types of resources such as manpower, machinery, and materials. ABC Construction Firm struggled with:

Over-allocation or under-allocation of resources, leading to idle time or bottlenecks.
Inaccurate estimations of resource needs, causing last-minute scrambles that increased costs.
Lack of real-time data to make adjustments in resource allocation during the project lifecycle.

The Solution

ABC Construction Firm decided to implement a machine learning-based resource allocation system. The system was designed to:

Analyze historical data from past projects to understand patterns in resource usage.
Use real-time data to make dynamic adjustments in resource allocation.
Provide actionable recommendations to project managers for optimal resource distribution.

Implementation
Data Collection and Model Training

The first phase involved gathering historical data from completed projects, including timelines, types and quantities of resources used, and project outcomes. This data was used to train a machine learning model capable of identifying optimal resource allocation patterns.

Real-time Monitoring and Dynamic Adjustment

The trained model was integrated into the firm's existing project management software. It continuously monitored real-time data on resource usage, project progress, and other relevant metrics. When it detected inefficiencies or impending shortages, it alerted the project managers.

Actionable Recommendations

The system was programmed to offer specific recommendations for resource reallocation. For example, if it detected that a crane was underutilized in one project and another project was facing a machinery shortage, it would suggest transferring the crane to where it was needed most.

Results
Cost Reduction

Within the first year of implementation, ABC Construction Firm saw a 20% reduction in resource-related costs. The machine learning algorithm's accurate predictions helped avoid over-purchasing and reduced idle time for both manpower and machinery.

Improved Efficiency

The system's real-time monitoring and dynamic adjustment capabilities allowed project managers to react quickly to emerging needs, reducing delays and improving overall project efficiency. Project completion rates improved by 15% in the first year.

Enhanced Decision-making
The machine learning system provided data-driven insights that enhanced the decision-making process. Project managers were more confident in their resource allocation decisions, leading to smoother project execution and better team morale.

Conclusion
The integration of machine learning algorithms for resource allocation proved to be a game-changer for ABC Construction Firm. By leveraging historical and real-time data, the firm was able to optimize the allocation of resources across multiple projects, leading to significant cost reductions and efficiency gains. This case study serves as a compelling example of how advanced technologies like machine learning can solve complex, real-world challenges in industries like construction.

Section 5: Tools and Software for AI-Driven Data Analysis

Popular AI Tools for Project Management

Project managers today have a plethora of Artificial Intelligence (AI) tools at their disposal to assist with data analysis, each offering a unique set of features, advantages, and drawbacks. These tools can transform the way project managers approach tasks like risk assessment, resource allocation, and stakeholder communication, among others.

One of the most popular tools in this domain is Microsoft's Azure Machine Learning. This platform provides a wide range of machine learning algorithms and is particularly user-friendly, making it accessible even for those without a strong background in data science. Azure Machine Learning excels in its integration capabilities; it can seamlessly connect with other Microsoft products like Power BI for data visualization or Microsoft Teams for collaboration. However, the downside is its cost, as the pricing can be prohibitive for smaller organizations. Additionally, being a Microsoft product, it tends to work best within the Microsoft ecosystem, which might not be ideal for companies using a diverse set of software solutions.

Another noteworthy tool is IBM's Watson Analytics. Known for its natural language processing capabilities, Watson allows project managers to query their data using natural language, making it easier to extract meaningful insights without having to understand complex query languages. Watson is particularly strong in predictive analytics, which can be invaluable for risk assessment and forecasting. However, Watson can be overwhelming for beginners due to its extensive range of features, and like Azure, it can be on the expensive side.

Tableau is another tool that, while not an AI tool in the strictest sense, offers robust data analytics and visualization capabilities that can be augmented with machine learning plugins. Tableau is known for its intuitive, drag-and-drop interface that allows users to create complex data visualizations with ease. Its primary advantage is its flexibility; it can integrate with a wide variety of data sources and is highly customizable. However, its machine learning capabilities are not as advanced as those of Azure or Watson, requiring plugins or additional tools for more complex analyses.

For project managers interested in open-source options, Python libraries like scikit-learn offer a high degree of customization and are widely used for machine learning tasks. These libraries are free to use and supported by a large community of developers, which means a wealth of tutorials and resources are available. However, they require a good understanding of both programming and data science concepts, making them less accessible for those without technical expertise.

Google's TensorFlow is another open-source option that offers more advanced machine learning capabilities. It's highly scalable, capable of handling large datasets, and is backed by Google's extensive infrastructure. However, TensorFlow has a steep learning curve and may be overkill for smaller projects or simpler analyses.

The choice of an AI tool for data analysis in project management will depend on a variety of factors including the specific needs of the project, the technical expertise of the team, and budget considerations. Tools like Azure Machine Learning and IBM Watson offer powerful, user-friendly platforms with a range of features but can be expensive. Tableau offers flexibility and ease of use for data visualization but may require additional tools for advanced machine learning tasks. Open-source options like scikit-learn and TensorFlow offer high customizability and are budget-friendly but require a higher degree of technical expertise.

Section 6: Ethical and Legal Considerations

Data Privacy and Security

The integration of Artificial Intelligence (AI) into project management has undeniably brought about a revolution in how projects are executed, monitored, and assessed. However, the use of AI for analyzing potentially sensitive project data introduces a new set of challenges around legal and ethical considerations, particularly concerning data privacy and security. Project managers, therefore, must tread carefully, ensuring that they are not only compliant with laws but also respectful of ethical boundaries.

Data privacy is one of the most pressing concerns when it comes to the use of AI in project management. Many projects involve the collection and analysis of sensitive information, such as personal data of team members or confidential business information. Laws like the General Data Protection Regulation (GDPR) in Europe have set stringent guidelines on how such data should be handled. Project managers must be fully aware of these regulations and ensure that any AI tools used for data analysis are compliant. This often means ensuring that data is anonymized before analysis and that it is stored securely, with access restricted to authorized personnel only.

Beyond legal compliance, there's an ethical obligation to respect the privacy of individuals whose data is being analyzed. Even if the law doesn't explicitly require it, best practices would dictate that informed consent should be obtained from team members or other stakeholders if their personal data will be subjected to AI analysis. Transparency is key; people have the right to know how their information will be used and what measures are in place to protect their privacy.

Security is another major concern. The use of AI often involves the transfer of large volumes of data to external servers for analysis, which could potentially expose sensitive information to cyber threats. Project managers must ensure that any AI tools they use employ robust security measures, such as end-to-end encryption and multi-factor authentication, to protect against data breaches. Regular security audits can also be beneficial to identify and address potential vulnerabilities.

Moreover, the use of AI in project management often involves third-party vendors who provide AI analytics services. In such cases, project managers must conduct thorough due diligence to ensure that these vendors are compliant with data privacy laws and follow best practices for data security. Contracts with vendors should clearly outline the responsibilities of each party in maintaining data privacy and security, and ideally, should be reviewed by legal experts specializing in data protection laws.

Another aspect to consider is the potential for algorithmic bias, where the AI system might make recommendations or predictions that are unfairly discriminatory. While this is more of an ethical than a legal concern, it's something that project managers need to be aware of. Ensuring that the data used to train AI algorithms is diverse and representative can mitigate this risk to some extent.

The use of AI in project management offers numerous benefits in terms of efficiency and data-driven decision-making. However, it also introduces significant legal and ethical challenges around data privacy and security. Project managers must be well-versed in relevant laws and ethical guidelines to ensure that they are using AI responsibly. This involves choosing compliant AI tools, securing informed consent where necessary, implementing robust security measures, and vetting third-party vendors rigorously. By taking these steps, project managers can harness the power of AI while also respecting the legal and ethical boundaries that come with it.

Algorithmic Accountability

The increasing integration of Artificial Intelligence (AI) into various sectors, including project management, healthcare, and finance, has raised important questions about responsibility and accountability, especially when an AI algorithm makes a wrong decision. The ethical implications of algorithmic decision-making are complex and multi-faceted, touching on issues of responsibility, transparency, and fairness.

At the most basic level, one could argue that the developers who created the algorithm are responsible for its actions. After all, the algorithm operates based on the rules and parameters set by its human creators. However, this perspective oversimplifies the issue. AI algorithms, particularly those based on machine learning, are not merely executing pre-defined rules; they are "learning" from data and making decisions that even their developers may not fully understand. This is especially true for deep learning algorithms, which can have millions of parameters and are often described as "black boxes" because their decision-making processes are not transparent.

Another perspective is to consider the responsibility of the organization that deployed the AI algorithm. In a project management context, for example, if an AI tool incorrectly assesses the risk level of a project, leading to financial loss, the organization might be held accountable for relying on an imperfect tool. This viewpoint suggests that organizations need to exercise due diligence when implementing AI solutions, ensuring they are thoroughly tested and their limitations understood.

However, placing the entire burden of responsibility on the deploying organization can also be problematic. It assumes that the organization has the expertise to fully understand the AI's decision-making process, which may not be the case. Furthermore, it doesn't account for situations where the AI's decision is influenced by biased or incorrect data that the organization did not provide.

This brings us to the issue of data responsibility. AI algorithms are only as good as the data they are trained on. If the algorithm makes a wrong decision based on flawed or biased data, who is responsible? The entity that provided the data? The developers who did not adequately clean or vet the data? Or the algorithm itself for not being robust enough to handle imperfect data?

The ethical implications extend beyond responsibility to include issues of transparency and fairness. If an AI algorithm makes a decision, stakeholders have a right to understand how that decision was made, especially if it has significant consequences. This is challenging with complex algorithms that are not easily interpretable. Moreover, there's the issue of fairness. If an algorithm makes a decision that disproportionately impacts a certain group of people, it raises ethical concerns even if the decision is technically "correct" based on the data.

Given these complexities, some experts advocate for a shared responsibility model, where accountability is distributed across the developers, the deploying organization, and even the entities providing the data. This model would require greater collaboration and transparency among all parties involved. Regulatory frameworks could also play a role, setting standards for AI accountability and requiring third-party audits of AI systems, especially those used in critical decision-making processes.

the question of who is responsible when an AI algorithm makes a wrong decision is fraught with ethical complexities. It touches on issues of accountability among developers, deploying organizations, and data providers, as well as broader concerns about transparency and fairness. A multi-faceted approach that includes shared responsibility, regulatory oversight, and greater emphasis on ethical considerations is crucial for addressing these challenges.

Conclusion: The Future of Data-Driven Decision Making in Project Management
The integration of AI into data analysis is not just a technological shift; it's a paradigm shift that has the potential to significantly enhance project outcomes. Project managers who adapt to this new data-driven landscape will be better equipped to lead successful projects in the future.

CHAPTER 4: AUTOMATING ROUTINE TASKS: AI IN SCHEDULING AND RESOURCE ALLOCATION

Introduction: The Challenge of Routine Tasks in Project Management

Project management is a multifaceted discipline that requires a delicate balance between strategic planning and day-to-day operations. While strategic decisions often get the spotlight, routine tasks like scheduling and resource allocation are the unsung heroes that keep a project on track. However, these tasks can be time-consuming and prone to human error. This chapter explores how AI can automate and optimize these routine tasks, freeing up project managers to focus on more complex and strategic aspects of their projects.

Section 1: The Traditional Landscape of Scheduling and Resource Allocation

The Importance of Scheduling and Resource Allocation

Effective scheduling and resource allocation are foundational elements that can make or break a project. They serve as the backbone of project management, dictating the flow of activities, the utilization of resources, and ultimately, the successful completion of the project within its defined scope, time, and cost constraints. The intricacies of these two aspects go beyond merely setting timelines or assigning tasks; they encompass a nuanced understanding of project objectives, team dynamics, resource capabilities, and even external variables like market conditions or regulatory changes.

Scheduling is not just about setting start and end dates for various tasks; it's a complex process that requires a deep understanding of task dependencies, milestones, critical paths, and potential bottlenecks. A well-crafted schedule serves as a roadmap for the entire team, providing a clear vision of the project's lifecycle. It helps in identifying which tasks are critical to project completion and which have some leeway in terms of time. This enables project managers to prioritize effectively, ensuring that resources are focused on activities that are crucial for meeting project deadlines.

Effective scheduling also involves contingency planning. No project unfolds exactly as planned; there are always unforeseen challenges or opportunities that arise. A robust schedule will account for such uncertainties by building in buffers or slack time, allowing for adjustments as the project progresses. This adaptability is essential for navigating through unexpected delays or accelerating activities when new resources become available.

Resource allocation, on the other hand, involves assigning the available resources—both human and material—in the most efficient way to complete the tasks outlined in the schedule. This is a dynamic process that requires continuous monitoring and adjustment. Over-allocation can lead to burnout and increased costs, while under-allocation can result in idle resources and project delays. Striking the right balance is crucial, and this is where the skill of the project manager comes into play.

Human resources, often the most complex to manage, require special attention. Team members come with varying skill sets, experience levels, and work preferences. Effective resource allocation involves matching these individual attributes to the specific requirements of tasks. It's not just about filling slots;

it's about optimizing the team composition for maximum productivity and job satisfaction, which in turn reduces turnover and boosts morale.

Material resources, such as equipment, software, or raw materials, also need to be managed efficiently. This involves not just the initial allocation but also ongoing tracking to ensure that they are being used effectively and are in good condition. Poor management of material resources can lead to wastage, increased costs, and even project failure if critical equipment breaks down or materials are unavailable when needed.

The integration of scheduling and resource allocation is vital. The schedule sets the framework within which resources are allocated, while the availability and capability of resources can influence the schedule. For example, if a key team member is unavailable for a certain period, tasks dependent on that individual may need to be rescheduled. Conversely, the acquisition of new material resources might accelerate certain tasks, allowing for a more aggressive schedule.

Effective scheduling and resource allocation are critical for project success. They provide the structured framework that guides the project from initiation to completion, ensuring that tasks are completed on time and resources are used efficiently. Beyond mere planning, they require ongoing monitoring and adjustment to adapt to the dynamic nature of projects. By mastering these aspects, project managers can significantly increase the likelihood of meeting project objectives, thereby ensuring success and stakeholder satisfaction.

The Limitations of Traditional Methods

Traditional methods of project management, which often rely on manual input and fixed algorithms, have been the mainstay for organizing and executing projects for many years. While these methods have their merits, they also come with a set of limitations that can hinder a project's success in today's fast-paced and ever-changing environment.

One of the most significant drawbacks of traditional methods is their rigidity. Fixed algorithms and manual processes are often set up at the beginning of a project and are expected to remain constant throughout its lifecycle. While this approach offers a sense of stability and predictability, it lacks the flexibility needed to adapt to changes. Projects are dynamic by nature; they are influenced by a myriad of variables including market conditions, technological advancements, and human factors, among others. A rigid system that cannot adapt to these changing variables is likely to become obsolete quickly, leading to inefficiencies and setbacks.

This rigidity is particularly problematic when there are changes in project scope. Scope changes are almost inevitable in most projects, whether due to new stakeholder requirements, unforeseen opportunities, or adjustments in project objectives. Traditional methods, with their fixed algorithms, struggle to accommodate these changes smoothly. Revising schedules, reallocating resources, and updating cost estimates often require manual intervention, which is not only time-consuming but also prone to errors. This can result in delays and cost overruns, affecting the overall success of the project.

Resource availability is another area where traditional methods fall short. In a manual system, tracking the availability and utilization of resources—be it human or material—can be a daunting task. Project managers may find themselves sifting through spreadsheets, emails, and reports to get a clear picture of resource allocation. This cumbersome process makes it difficult to make quick adjustments, leading to either resource wastage or bottlenecks. For instance, a team member might be underutilized because the project manager wasn't aware of their availability, or a critical piece of equipment might sit idle because its usage wasn't adequately planned.

Unforeseen challenges are another aspect where traditional methods show their limitations. Every project encounters unexpected issues, ranging from minor setbacks to major crises. These could be anything from a key team member falling ill to a critical supplier going bankrupt. Traditional project management methods, with their fixed algorithms and manual processes, are often ill-equipped to respond to these challenges swiftly. The time taken to manually reassess and adjust plans can exacerbate the problem, turning a manageable issue into a significant crisis.

Moreover, the time-consuming nature of traditional methods can itself be a drawback. Time is often of the essence in projects, and delays in decision-making can have a cascading effect on timelines, costs, and even project quality. The manual input required for tasks like data collection, analysis, and reporting can consume valuable time that could be better spent on more strategic activities. This inefficiency is not just a drain on time but also on human resources, as team members who are tied up with manual tasks are unable to focus on their core responsibilities.

While traditional methods of project management have served us well for many years, they come with inherent limitations in today's dynamic and complex project environments. Their rigidity, time-consuming processes, and inability to adapt to changes in project scope, resource availability, and unforeseen challenges can hinder a project's success. As projects continue to evolve in complexity and stakeholders demand greater efficiency and adaptability, there is a growing need for more flexible and responsive project management approaches.

Section 2: The AI Revolution in Routine Task Management

How AI Can Automate Scheduling

The advent of Artificial Intelligence (AI) in project management has opened up new avenues for automating and optimizing various aspects of project execution, one of which is scheduling. Traditional scheduling methods, often manual and rigid, have limitations in handling the dynamic and multifaceted nature of modern projects. AI algorithms, on the other hand, offer a more sophisticated and adaptive approach, capable of analyzing a multitude of variables to automatically generate optimized schedules.

One of the most significant advantages of using AI for scheduling is its ability to handle complex data sets. In any given project, there are numerous variables that can influence the schedule, ranging from team availability and task complexity to historical data on past projects. Manually analyzing these variables to create an optimized schedule can be a Herculean task, requiring hours of effort and a high level of expertise. AI algorithms can perform this analysis in a fraction of the time, sifting through large volumes of data to identify patterns, correlations, and dependencies that may not be apparent to a human project manager.

Take, for example, the variable of team availability. In a complex project with multiple team members having different skill sets, availability constraints, and work preferences, scheduling can become a logistical nightmare. AI algorithms can automatically factor in these individual constraints, analyzing data from calendars, past performance metrics, and even personal preferences to allocate tasks in a way that maximizes productivity while respecting individual availability. This not only ensures that tasks are allocated to the most suitable team members but also that the team members are engaged and satisfied, leading to better performance and lower turnover.

Task complexity is another variable that AI algorithms can analyze effectively. Different tasks within a project can vary widely in terms of complexity, duration, and required resources. AI can analyze historical data and current project metrics to estimate the complexity of each task accurately. This enables more realistic scheduling, as tasks that are more complex can be allocated additional time and resources, ensuring that they don't become bottlenecks that delay the entire project.

Historical data provides a goldmine of information that can be used to optimize scheduling, and this is where AI truly shines. By analyzing data from past projects, AI algorithms can identify trends and patterns that can inform the current schedule. For instance, if the data shows that a particular phase of similar past projects consistently took longer than initially estimated, the AI can adjust the schedule to allocate more time for that phase. This kind of predictive scheduling can be incredibly valuable in avoiding delays and cost overruns.

Moreover, AI algorithms can adapt in real-time as the project progresses. If there are changes in team availability, unexpected delays, or even early completions of certain tasks, the AI can automatically update the schedule to reflect these changes. This real-time adaptability is crucial for keeping the project on track, allowing for quick course corrections without requiring manual intervention.

AI algorithms offer a transformative approach to project scheduling, capable of analyzing a multitude of complex variables to generate optimized schedules automatically. By factoring in team availability, task complexity, and historical data, AI provides a more accurate, efficient, and adaptive scheduling solution. This not only enhances project execution but also frees up the project manager to focus on more strategic aspects of the project, ultimately contributing to better project outcomes.

AI in Resource Allocation

The application of machine learning algorithms in project management has ushered in a new era of efficiency and precision, particularly in the area of resource allocation. Traditional methods of allocating resources often rely on static models and manual adjustments, which can be both time-consuming and error-prone. Machine learning algorithms, however, can dynamically predict the optimal allocation of resources based on a variety of factors such as past performance, current workload, and future projections. Moreover, these algorithms are capable of making real-time adjustments as conditions change, ensuring that the project remains on track and resources are utilized most effectively.

One of the most compelling advantages of using machine learning for resource allocation is its ability to learn from past performance. By analyzing historical data from completed projects, machine learning algorithms can identify patterns and trends that can inform future resource allocation. For example, if the algorithm detects that certain types of tasks consistently take longer than initially estimated, it can automatically allocate additional resources to similar tasks in future projects. Similarly, if certain team members have demonstrated high efficiency in specific tasks, the algorithm can prioritize assigning similar tasks to those individuals, thereby maximizing productivity.

Current workload is another critical factor that machine learning algorithms can analyze for optimal resource allocation. In a dynamic project environment, workloads can fluctuate due to various factors such as changes in project scope, unexpected delays, or early completion of tasks. Machine learning algorithms can continuously monitor the current workload across different resources—be it team members, equipment, or materials—and make adjustments in real-time. For instance, if a team member finishes a task ahead of schedule, the algorithm can immediately reassign them to another task that requires attention, thereby reducing idle time. Conversely, if a piece of critical equipment breaks down, the algorithm can instantly redistribute tasks to other available resources to minimize delays.

Future projections add another layer of sophistication to machine learning-based resource allocation. By analyzing current and historical data, machine learning algorithms can make informed predictions about future conditions that may affect resource allocation. These could range from anticipated changes in team availability due to planned vacations or training programs to seasonal fluctuations in resource costs. By factoring in these future projections, the algorithm can preemptively adjust resource allocation plans, ensuring that the project is not caught off guard by foreseeable changes.

The real power of machine learning algorithms lies in their ability to make real-time adjustments. Unlike traditional methods, which often require manual intervention to update resource allocation plans, machine learning algorithms can automatically adjust to changing conditions. Whether it's an unexpected resource constraint, a sudden change in project scope, or even an unplanned opportunity to accelerate certain tasks, the algorithm can instantly update the resource allocation plan to optimize for these new conditions. This real-time adaptability is invaluable in today's fast-paced project environments, where conditions can change rapidly and the cost of delays can be significant.

Machine learning algorithms offer a dynamic and adaptive approach to resource allocation that far surpasses the capabilities of traditional methods. By analyzing past performance, current workload, and future projections, these algorithms can predict the optimal allocation of resources with a high degree of accuracy. Their ability to make real-time adjustments ensures that the project can adapt to changing conditions efficiently, thereby maximizing resource utilization, reducing costs, and improving project outcomes.

Section 3: Practical Applications and Benefits

Real-time Adaptability

The dynamic nature of project environments makes adaptability a crucial element for successful project management. Traditional methods often struggle to keep pace with real-time changes, requiring manual intervention to update schedules and reallocate resources, which can be both time-consuming and error-prone. Artificial Intelligence (AI) algorithms offer a transformative solution to this challenge, providing the ability to adapt to real-time changes automatically, thereby ensuring that projects remain agile and efficient.

One of the most significant advantages of AI algorithms in project management is their capability to continuously monitor a multitude of variables that impact the project. These could range from team availability and task completion rates to external factors like market conditions or regulatory changes. By constantly analyzing this data, AI algorithms can detect shifts in the project environment as they happen, enabling immediate action.

For instance, consider a scenario where a key team member unexpectedly falls ill, creating a sudden resource gap. An AI algorithm can instantly identify this change and assess its impact on the project schedule. It can then automatically update the schedule to redistribute tasks among available team members, ensuring that critical milestones are still met. If the algorithm determines that the resource gap cannot be filled internally, it might even trigger alerts for temporary external hiring, thereby minimizing delays.

Real-time adaptability is not just about responding to challenges; it's also about capitalizing on unexpected opportunities. For example, if a particular phase of the project is completed ahead of schedule, AI algorithms can immediately reallocate resources to other tasks that are lagging behind or to new tasks that can now be initiated sooner than planned. This ensures that the gained time is not wasted but is effectively used to accelerate other parts of the project.

AI algorithms can also adapt to more subtle, gradual changes in the project environment. For example, if the algorithm detects a consistent improvement in the efficiency of a particular team or the frequent early completion of a specific type of task, it can update future schedules to reflect this increased efficiency. This kind of ongoing optimization ensures that the project is always operating at peak efficiency, adapting to both the strengths and weaknesses that become apparent as the project progresses.

The ability of AI algorithms to make real-time adjustments extends beyond just scheduling to include resource allocation as well. For instance, if the algorithm detects that certain resources are being underutilized—be it human resources, equipment, or materials—it can automatically reallocate them to tasks where they can be more effective. This ensures optimal resource utilization, reducing costs, and improving project outcomes.

Moreover, the adaptability of AI algorithms is not limited to individual projects. In organizations where multiple projects are running concurrently, AI can provide a holistic optimization strategy. If a resource is idle in one project and needed in another, the algorithm can facilitate a cross-project reallocation, thereby maximizing overall organizational efficiency.

The ability of AI algorithms to adapt to real-time changes in the project environment represents a paradigm shift in project management. By continuously monitoring various project variables and making automatic adjustments to schedules and resource allocation, AI ensures that projects are agile, resilient, and efficient. This real-time adaptability minimizes the impact of unexpected challenges, capitalizes on unforeseen opportunities, and enables ongoing optimization, thereby significantly enhancing the likelihood of project success.

Increased Efficiency and Cost Savings

In the realm of project management, cost overruns are a common issue that can jeopardize the success of a project. One of the key factors contributing to cost inefficiency is poor scheduling and resource allocation. Automated, optimized scheduling and resource allocation, facilitated by advanced technologies like Artificial Intelligence (AI) and machine learning, can dramatically improve this aspect of project management. By reducing idle time and ensuring that resources are used to their full potential, these automated systems can lead to significant cost savings, thereby enhancing the overall viability and success of projects.

Idle time is one of the most glaring sources of cost inefficiency in projects. Whether it's a team member waiting for tasks, equipment lying unused, or materials being stored for extended periods, idle time is essentially wasted time that incurs costs without contributing to project progress. Automated scheduling algorithms can significantly reduce idle time by dynamically matching tasks with available resources. For instance, if a team member completes a task ahead of schedule, the algorithm can automatically assign them a new task, thereby reducing the time they spend idle. This not only speeds up project completion but also maximizes the return on human resources.

Similarly, automated systems can optimize the use of material resources and equipment. Traditional methods often involve bulk ordering of materials or booking equipment way in advance to avoid potential shortages. While this approach ensures availability, it also leads to extended periods where these resources are idle, incurring storage costs and the risk of obsolescence or degradation. Automated systems can predict the exact timing and quantity of resources needed, allowing for just-in-time procurement and usage. This minimizes idle time for material resources and equipment, thereby reducing associated costs.

Ensuring that resources are used to their full potential is another avenue for cost savings. In traditional project management, resource allocation is often done based on rough estimates and generalizations, which can lead to either over-allocation or under-allocation. Over-allocation results in wasted resources, while under-allocation leads to project delays, both of which incur additional costs. Automated, optimized resource allocation algorithms can analyze a multitude of factors, such as task complexity, team skills, historical performance, and even real-time progress, to allocate resources most efficiently. By matching the right amount and type of resources to each task, these algorithms ensure that resources are used to their full potential, thereby maximizing efficiency and minimizing waste.

The cost savings from automated, optimized scheduling and resource allocation are not just theoretical; they have a tangible impact on the project's bottom line. Reduced idle time and more efficient resource utilization directly translate to lower operational costs. Additionally, by speeding up project completion and reducing the likelihood of delays, automated systems can also lead to indirect cost savings. Faster project turnaround means quicker realization of project benefits, whether it's revenue generation for a commercial project or social impact for a community project. It also enhances the organization's reputation for efficiency and reliability, leading to potential long-term gains through increased client trust and market competitiveness.

Automated, optimized scheduling and resource allocation offer a powerful strategy for cost reduction in project management. By leveraging advanced algorithms to reduce idle time and ensure that resources are used to their full potential, these systems can lead to significant cost savings. These savings not only make projects more financially viable but also contribute to faster, more efficient project execution, thereby amplifying the overall success and impact of the project.

Section 4: Case Studies

Case Study 1: AI in Manufacturing Scheduling

Background
ABC Manufacturing Co. is a mid-sized company specializing in the production of automotive parts. Despite having a robust production line and skilled workforce, the company faced challenges in optimizing its production schedules. The traditional methods employed were increasingly proving to be inefficient, leading to delays, resource wastage, and ultimately, a loss in competitiveness. After a thorough evaluation of potential solutions, the company decided to implement an AI-driven scheduling system to optimize its production processes.

Objectives
The primary objective was to increase production efficiency by at least 15% within the first year of implementing the AI system. Secondary objectives included reducing idle time for both machinery and workforce, improving resource allocation, and minimizing production delays.

Implementation
ABC Manufacturing Co. partnered with XYZ Tech, a leading provider of AI solutions for manufacturing, to develop and implement a customized AI-driven scheduling system. The system was designed to analyze a multitude of variables, including machine availability, workforce skills, raw material inventory, and historical production data. After a three-month pilot phase, the system was rolled out across the entire production line.

Results
Within the first six months of implementation, ABC Manufacturing Co. observed a significant improvement in its production efficiency. Key results included:

- A 20% increase in overall production efficiency, surpassing the initial target of 15%.
- A 30% reduction in machinery idle time, leading to lower energy consumption and

---

maintenance costs.
- A 25% reduction in workforce idle time, allowing for better labor cost management.
- A 10% reduction in production delays, leading to improved customer satisfaction and retention.

Ethical and Legal Considerations

Given that the AI system used employee data for optimizing schedules, ABC Manufacturing Co. took several steps to ensure ethical and legal compliance. All employees were informed about the new system and how their data would be used, and consent was obtained. The company also implemented robust data security measures to protect employee information. Regular audits were conducted to ensure compliance with data privacy laws and to check for any signs of algorithmic bias.

Lessons Learned and Future Directions

The success of the AI-driven scheduling system has made ABC Manufacturing Co. consider other areas where AI can be implemented for further efficiency gains, such as in supply chain management and quality control. One key lesson learned was the importance of employee training and change management in ensuring the successful adoption of new technologies.

Conclusion

The implementation of an AI-driven scheduling system at ABC Manufacturing Co. led to significant improvements in production efficiency, far exceeding the company's initial objectives. This case study serves as a compelling example of how AI can be effectively leveraged to solve specific operational challenges in manufacturing, provided that ethical and legal considerations are adequately addressed.

Case Study 2: AI in IT Project Resource Allocation

Introduction

DEF IT Solutions is a leading IT services company specializing in software development and cloud computing solutions. Despite its success, the company faced ongoing challenges in resource allocation across its various projects. Traditional methods were falling short, leading to inefficiencies, increased project costs, and missed deadlines. To address these issues, DEF IT Solutions decided to implement machine learning algorithms designed to optimize resource allocation.

Objectives

The primary goal was to reduce project costs by at least 10% within the first year of implementing the machine learning algorithms. Additional objectives included improving project completion rates, reducing resource idle time, and enhancing client satisfaction.

Implementation Strategy

DEF IT Solutions collaborated with GHI Analytics, a firm specializing in machine learning solutions for business applications. Together, they developed a machine learning algorithm tailored to DEF's specific needs. The algorithm was designed to analyze various factors, such as employee skill sets, project requirements, historical performance data, and real-time project status. After a two-month testing phase on smaller projects, the algorithm was integrated into the company's main project management system.

Results

The results were both immediate and significant:

- Project costs were reduced by 15%, exceeding the initial target of 10%.
- Resource idle time was cut by 20%, leading to better utilization of both human and technical resources.
- Project completion rates improved by 8%, resulting in higher client satisfaction and increased repeat business.
- The algorithm also identified opportunities for cross-training staff, leading to a more versatile and adaptive workforce.

Ethical and Legal Compliance

Given that the machine learning algorithm used personal employee data to make resource allocation decisions, DEF IT Solutions took several steps to ensure compliance with data privacy regulations. Employees were informed about how their data would be used and explicit consent was obtained. The company also strengthened its cybersecurity measures to protect this sensitive data. Regular audits were conducted to ensure ongoing compliance and to check for any potential biases in the algorithm's decision-making.

Lessons Learned and Future Directions

The success of this initiative has encouraged DEF IT Solutions to explore other machine learning applications, including automated customer service solutions and predictive maintenance for their internal IT infrastructure. One important lesson learned was the need for ongoing monitoring and adjustment of the machine learning algorithm to adapt to changing project dynamics and workforce composition.

Conclusion

The implementation of machine learning algorithms for resource allocation at DEF IT Solutions led to substantial cost savings and operational improvements. This case study demonstrates the potential of machine learning to significantly enhance project management and resource allocation, provided that ethical and legal considerations are carefully managed. The experience of DEF IT Solutions serves as a valuable blueprint for other IT companies looking to leverage advanced technology to solve complex operational challenges.

Section 5: Tools and Platforms for AI-Driven Scheduling and Resource Allocation

Overview of Available Tools

Smartsheet with its AI Scheduling Add-on offers a cloud-based platform that integrates seamlessly with dynamic Gantt charts for visual scheduling. It also provides real-time resource allocation based on team availability and skill sets, along with predictive analytics for risk assessment. One of the major advantages of Smartsheet is its user-friendly interface, which requires minimal training. It also integrates seamlessly with other project management tools and software, and its real-time updates allow for immediate adjustments to schedules and resources. However, the AI add-on comes at an additional cost over the basic Smartsheet subscription, and the platform has limited offline capabilities.

Clarizen with its AI Resource Optimizer focuses on maximizing resource utilization. It features automated matching of tasks with the most suitable resources based on historical performance and real-time tracking of resource utilization rates. It also offers scenario planning for "what-if" analysis. Clarizen is highly customizable to fit specific project needs and has excellent reporting capabilities with in-depth analytics. It also allows for cross-project resource allocation. However, it has a steeper learning curve compared to other tools, and its higher cost can be a barrier for smaller organizations.

Microsoft Project with AI-driven Scheduling integrates AI algorithms into its already robust project management software. It offers features for optimizing task sequencing and duration and provides real-time collaboration features. It also integrates with the Microsoft 365 suite for enhanced functionality. One of the pros of using Microsoft Project is its familiar interface for those already using Microsoft products. It also offers strong security features, including data encryption and multi-factor authentication, and has extensive support and training resources. However, the tool can be overwhelming for smaller projects due to its extensive features and requires a separate Microsoft 365 subscription for full functionality.

Asana with AI Workload Management focuses on balancing workloads across team members to ensure optimal productivity. It uses machine learning algorithms to analyze past performance and predict future workloads, thereby enabling more accurate resource allocation. Asana is known for its intuitive user interface and robust collaboration features, making it easy for teams to stay aligned. It also offers integration with a wide range of third-party apps and services. However, its AI features are part of the more expensive Business and Enterprise plans, making it less accessible for smaller teams or organizations on a budget.

Each of these AI tools offers a unique set of features designed to automate and optimize scheduling and resource allocation in project management. While they all offer significant advantages in terms of efficiency and adaptability, they also come with their own limitations, such as cost, learning curve, and integration with other tools. Therefore, when choosing an AI tool for project management, it's important to consider not just its capabilities but also how well it aligns with the specific needs and constraints of your project or organization.

Section 6: Ethical and Social Considerations

Job Displacement Concerns

The integration of Artificial Intelligence into various industries has been a double-edged sword. On one hand, AI's capability to automate routine tasks has led to unprecedented levels of efficiency and productivity. On the other hand, this automation has raised valid concerns about job displacement, particularly for roles that have traditionally focused on these routine tasks.

AI's prowess in handling repetitive, time-consuming tasks is undeniable. From data entry and analysis to scheduling and resource allocation, AI algorithms can perform these tasks with a speed and accuracy that far surpass human capabilities. This automation frees up human workers to focus on more complex, creative tasks that require emotional intelligence, critical thinking, and nuanced decision-making—areas where AI still falls short. In this sense, AI can be seen as a complementary force that augments human capabilities, allowing for a more effective and streamlined workflow.

However, the flip side of this automation is the potential for job displacement. Roles that have traditionally been centered around routine tasks are the most vulnerable. For example, administrative roles that involve a lot of data entry, scheduling, and basic reporting may see a significant reduction in demand as AI systems take over these responsibilities. Similarly, in project management, tasks like basic data analysis, risk assessment, and resource allocation could increasingly become automated, reducing the need for human intervention.

The concern about job displacement isn't just about the loss of jobs but also about the transition challenges that come with it. Not everyone can easily move from a role focused on routine tasks to one that requires more complex skills. Reskilling and upskilling are often cited as solutions, but these are not straightforward paths. They require time, investment, and a conducive learning environment, which may not be accessible to everyone. Moreover, there's the psychological and emotional toll of job insecurity and the stress of having to adapt to rapidly changing job requirements.

It's also worth noting that while AI can handle complex calculations and data analysis, the interpretation of that data still largely relies on human expertise. The context in which data exists, the ethical considerations surrounding its use, and the strategic decisions that are made based on data analysis are areas where human judgment is irreplaceable. So, while the tasks may change, the need for human expertise and decision-making remains, albeit in a different capacity.

While AI's ability to handle routine tasks brings with it the promise of increased efficiency and the opportunity for human workers to engage in more meaningful work, it also raises serious concerns about job displacement. The challenge lies in finding a balance where AI can be leveraged for its strengths without leading to a significant negative impact on employment. This may involve a combination of reskilling programs, policy interventions, and thoughtful implementation of AI that considers not just the economic but also the human impact.

Data Privacy

The integration of Artificial Intelligence into scheduling and resource allocation has brought about a revolution in efficiency and productivity. However, this transformation comes with its own set of challenges, particularly concerning the ethical and legal dimensions of data privacy. To optimize scheduling and resource allocation, AI algorithms require access to a wealth of employee data. This data can range from basic information like work hours and job roles to more sensitive metrics like performance reviews, skill assessments, and even interpersonal dynamics within a team. While the analysis of this data can lead to highly efficient project management, it also opens a Pandora's box of privacy concerns.

One of the primary issues is the extent to which employees are aware that their data is being collected and analyzed. Transparency is a cornerstone of ethical data usage, but in the rush to implement AI solutions, the lines of what is acceptable and what is not can sometimes become blurred. Employees have a right to know not just that their data is being used but also how it's being used and for what specific purposes. Without clear communication and consent, the use of AI in this context can become ethically murky.

Moreover, the storage and security of this sensitive data become paramount. Data breaches are a growing concern across all sectors, and the leakage of employee data could have severe repercussions, both for the individuals involved and for the organization. The ethical responsibility extends to ensuring that adequate security measures are in place to protect this data from unauthorized access or hacking.

Legal considerations also come into play, especially given the varying regulations around data privacy in different jurisdictions. Laws such as the General Data Protection Regulation (GDPR) in Europe have stringent requirements for data collection and usage. Non-compliance with such regulations not only exposes organizations to legal repercussions but can also severely damage their reputation. Therefore, it's crucial for organizations to be aware of and compliant with the data privacy laws that apply to them, which may even involve navigating a complex web of regulations if they operate in multiple jurisdictions.

The ethical and legal challenges extend to the algorithms themselves. There's a growing awareness of the potential for algorithmic bias, where the AI systems reflect the conscious or unconscious biases of their human creators or the historical data they were trained on. In the context of scheduling and resource allocation, such biases could lead to unfair or discriminatory practices. For instance, if an algorithm were trained on data from an environment where certain groups were historically underrepresented or marginalized, it might perpetuate those biases in its scheduling and resource allocation decisions.

While the use of AI in scheduling and resource allocation offers significant benefits in terms of efficiency and productivity, it also raises complex ethical and legal questions around data privacy. These concerns span issues of transparency, consent, data security, legal compliance, and even the potential for algorithmic bias. As organizations increasingly adopt AI for project management, it's imperative that they address these issues proactively, balancing the drive for efficiency with the ethical and legal responsibilities they have toward their employees.

Conclusion: The Future is Automated

As AI technologies continue to advance, their application in automating routine tasks in project management will become more widespread. Project managers who embrace these technologies will not only make their projects more efficient but also free up their time to focus on strategic decision-making, ultimately leading to more successful project outcomes.

CHAPTER 5: ENHANCING TEAM COLLABORATION AND COMMUNICATION WITH AI

Introduction: The Pillars of Team Collaboration and Communication

In any project, effective team collaboration and communication are vital for success. These elements are often the glue that holds a project together, ensuring that everyone is aligned and working toward common goals. However, as projects grow in complexity and teams become more distributed, maintaining effective communication and collaboration becomes increasingly challenging. This chapter delves into how AI can be leveraged to enhance these crucial aspects of project management.

Section 1: The Traditional Landscape of Team Collaboration and Communication

The Role of Communication in Project Success

Communication is often described as the backbone of any project, and for good reason. It serves as the conduit through which information flows, connecting various aspects of a project from planning and execution to monitoring and closure. In essence, communication is the glue that holds a project together, affecting everything from team morale to the execution of tasks. When communication is clear, consistent, and effective, it creates an environment where tasks are understood, milestones are clear, and team members feel valued and included. This, in turn, fosters a sense of collective ownership and accountability, which are critical for the successful completion of a project.

However, the absence of effective communication can have the opposite effect, leading to a cascade of issues that can jeopardize the success of the entire project. One of the most immediate impacts of poor communication is misunderstandings. When project objectives, individual tasks, or deadlines are not communicated clearly, it creates ambiguity. Team members may not fully understand what is expected of them, leading to errors, rework, and inefficiencies. This lack of clarity can also extend to interactions with stakeholders, clients, and even within the project team, causing misalignment and conflicting priorities.

Misunderstandings due to poor communication can also lead to delays. In a project environment where timelines are often tight, any delay can have a domino effect on subsequent tasks and phases. For example, if a team member misunderstands the specifications of a task and completes it incorrectly, it will require additional time to correct the mistake. This delay can push back other tasks that are dependent on the completion of the initial task, causing a ripple effect that can lead to missed deadlines and increased costs.

Poor communication also has a more subtle, yet equally damaging, impact on team morale. When communication is inconsistent or unclear, it can lead to frustration and disengagement among team members. This decline in morale can further exacerbate communication issues, creating a vicious cycle that is difficult to break. A disengaged team is less likely to collaborate effectively, share critical information, or address issues proactively, all of which are essential for the successful execution of a project.

Ultimately, poor communication can lead to project failure. Whether it's through misunderstandings that lead to incorrect task execution, delays that result in missed deadlines, or low morale that stifles productivity, the effects of poor communication are both pervasive and damaging. It undermines the very foundation on which the project is built, making it difficult, if not impossible, to achieve the project's objectives.

Communication is not just a peripheral aspect of project management; it's a critical success factor that permeates every element of a project. Effective communication ensures that everyone is aligned, engaged, and working toward the same goals, thereby increasing the likelihood of project success. Conversely, poor communication can lead to a host of problems, from misunderstandings and delays to low morale and project failure. Therefore, investing in clear, consistent, and effective communication is not just good practice; it's essential for the success of any project.

Challenges in Modern Team Collaboration

In today's globalized world, the landscape of project management has evolved to include teams that are often dispersed across multiple locations and time zones. While this geographical spread allows companies to tap into diverse skill sets and markets, it also introduces a layer of complexity to the already challenging task of effective communication. The traditional face-to-face interactions that facilitate clear and immediate understanding are often replaced by virtual meetings and written communications, each with its own set of limitations and potential for misunderstandings.

The challenge of time zones cannot be overstated. When team members are working hours that barely overlap, finding a suitable time for everyone to meet and discuss project updates becomes a logistical puzzle. Even when a meeting time is agreed upon, the team members attending outside of their regular working hours may not be as alert or engaged, affecting the quality of communication. The asynchronous nature of such global teams also means that immediate feedback or clarification on tasks is not always possible, leading to delays and potential errors.

Adding to the complexity is the sheer volume of communications that team members have to manage. In an effort to keep everyone updated, there's often a deluge of emails, instant messages, and notifications from project management software. Each of these communications demands attention and response, creating a constant stream of information that can be overwhelming to navigate. The risk here is twofold: important information may be lost in the noise, and team members may experience burnout from the constant need to stay connected.

This high volume of communications also increases the likelihood of misinterpretation, especially when team members come from different cultural backgrounds. What is considered a straightforward statement in one culture may be perceived as rude or ambiguous in another. Virtual communications, such as emails and messages, lack the non-verbal cues that help in understanding the context or emotional tone of a statement. This absence can lead to misunderstandings that are only magnified when cultural differences are also in play.

Moreover, the reliance on written communication in virtual teams can lead to delays in project execution. Writing is generally a slower process than speaking, and written communications often require additional time for review and editing to ensure clarity and accuracy. This time adds up, especially when multiple rounds of clarification are needed, leading to inefficiencies that could have been avoided in a face-to-face conversation.

In such a complex environment, effective communication requires more than just the exchange of information. It demands a well-thought-out strategy that considers the unique challenges of a global, virtual team. This may include the use of specialized project management and communication tools designed for virtual collaboration, scheduling regular check-ins to accommodate different time zones, and perhaps most importantly, fostering a culture of open communication where team members feel comfortable seeking clarification and providing feedback.

The globalization of teams brings with it the promise of diversity and access to a broader talent pool, but it also complicates the already challenging task of effective communication. The hurdles of multiple time zones, the overwhelming volume of communications, and the limitations of virtual interactions make it essential for project managers to be proactive and strategic in facilitating clear, effective communication. Without this, even the most promising projects can become mired in misunderstandings, delays, and inefficiencies.

Section 2: How AI is Transforming Team Collaboration and Communication

AI-Driven Communication Platforms

Artificial Intelligence has the potential to revolutionize the way we communicate, especially in the context of project management for global teams. As teams become more dispersed, spanning multiple locations and time zones, the challenges of effective communication multiply. AI can address some of these challenges by powering intelligent communication platforms designed to streamline interactions, improve efficiency, and reduce misunderstandings.

One of the most immediate benefits of AI in communication is its ability to prioritize and filter messages. In a typical project environment, team members are inundated with a constant stream of emails, messages, and notifications. This deluge of information can be overwhelming, leading to missed deadlines or overlooked details. AI algorithms can analyze the content, context, and urgency of incoming messages to prioritize them accordingly. For example, messages related to impending deadlines or critical issues can be flagged and moved to the top of a team member's inbox, ensuring that important communications receive timely attention. This not only helps in managing the volume of communications but also in reducing the cognitive load on team members, allowing them to focus on tasks that require their expertise.

Scheduling is another area where AI can have a significant impact. Finding a suitable time for a meeting that accommodates team members across different time zones is a complex task. AI algorithms can analyze the work schedules, time zones, and even the historical meeting attendance data of team members to suggest optimal times for meetings. These algorithms can also take into account the nature and urgency of the meeting to recommend a time that ensures maximum attendance and engagement. By automating this process, AI frees up valuable time that can be better spent on more strategic aspects of project management.

For global teams, language barriers can be a significant impediment to effective communication. Real-time translation services powered by AI can break down these barriers, allowing team members to communicate seamlessly regardless of their native language. Advanced Natural Language Processing (NLP) algorithms can provide accurate, real-time translations during virtual meetings, making it easier for team members to understand and contribute to the discussion. These algorithms can also translate written documents and messages, ensuring that all team members have access to the information they need, in a language they understand.

Moreover, AI-powered platforms can offer additional features like sentiment analysis to gauge the emotional tone of written communications. This can be particularly useful in virtual teams where non-verbal cues are absent. By analyzing the choice of words, sentence structure, and other linguistic elements, AI can provide insights into the emotional tone of a message, helping to prevent misunderstandings that could arise from cultural differences or the limitations of written communication.

AI has the potential to significantly enhance the effectiveness of communication within project teams, particularly those that are geographically dispersed. By intelligently prioritizing and filtering messages, automating the scheduling of meetings, providing real-time translation services, and even offering insights into emotional tones, AI-powered communication platforms can address many of the challenges that come with managing a global team. These capabilities not only improve the efficiency and accuracy of communications but also contribute to building a more inclusive and collaborative project environment.

Collaborative AI Tools for Teamwork

Artificial Intelligence is increasingly becoming a cornerstone in enhancing collaboration tools, particularly in the realm of project management software. One of the most straightforward yet impactful ways AI contributes is by automating routine updates. In a typical project environment, a considerable amount of time is spent on updating task statuses, logging hours, and keeping track of milestones. AI can automate these routine but essential updates by pulling data from various sources, analyzing it, and then updating the project dashboard in real-time. This automation not only saves time but also ensures that the project status is always current, providing a reliable basis for decision-making.

Beyond automating updates, AI can play a proactive role in flagging important issues that require immediate attention. For example, if a particular task is falling behind schedule, AI algorithms can analyze the delay's potential impact on other tasks and the overall project timeline. If the analysis reveals that the delay could lead to a critical bottleneck, the issue is flagged for immediate attention by the project manager. This proactive approach allows for timely intervention, reducing the risk of project delays and cost overruns.

AI's capabilities extend to optimizing task assignments as well. Traditional methods of task assignment often rely on project managers' intuition and experience, which, while valuable, can be subjective and prone to oversight. AI algorithms can analyze a range of factors, including team members' skills, past performance, and current workload, to suggest optimal task assignments. For instance, if a complex coding task arises in a software development project, the AI system can scan through historical data to identify team members who have successfully completed similar tasks in the past. It can also consider their current workload to ensure that they have the capacity to take on the new task. This data-driven approach to task assignment not only maximizes the chances of successful task completion but also contributes to more equitable distribution of work, thereby improving team morale.

The integration of AI into project management software thus serves to elevate the entire project management process. By automating routine updates, the system ensures that project data is always current and reliable. By proactively flagging issues, it allows for timely interventions that can save both time and money. And by optimizing task assignments, it ensures that the right people are working on the right tasks, maximizing both efficiency and job satisfaction. In doing so, AI transforms project management software from a passive tool for tracking progress into an active participant in the project, one that offers valuable insights and suggestions that can significantly improve project outcomes.

Section 3: Practical Applications and Benefits

Enhanced Decision-Making

Artificial Intelligence has the capability to delve into the intricacies of communication patterns within a team, offering a level of analysis that goes beyond what is immediately observable. By analyzing data from various communication channels—be it emails, chat logs, or even voice recordings from meetings—AI can identify patterns that may not be apparent even to the most experienced project managers. This kind of analysis can be invaluable in identifying bottlenecks or disconnects within a team, which, if left unaddressed, can have a detrimental impact on both team dynamics and decision-making.

Consider the issue of bottlenecks, where the flow of information or decision-making gets stalled at a particular point. Traditional methods of identifying bottlenecks often rely on self-reporting or are reactive in nature, becoming apparent only after they have caused a delay or problem. AI can proactively identify such bottlenecks by analyzing who is communicating with whom, how frequently, and about what topics. If, for example, all communication about a particular project phase is funneled through a single team member who is also involved in multiple other tasks, the AI system can flag this as a potential bottleneck. This allows for preemptive action, such as redistributing responsibilities to ensure smoother flow of information and faster decision-making.

Disconnects within a team are another issue that AI can help identify. These are instances where certain team members are not in sync with the rest of the group, either because they are not receiving all the necessary information, or their input is not being considered in decision-making. Such disconnects can lead to feelings of exclusion and can affect the quality of the work. AI can identify these disconnects by analyzing the frequency and quality of interactions between team members. For instance, if a team member's contributions in meetings are consistently overlooked or if they are not included in important email threads, these patterns can be flagged for further investigation.

What makes AI particularly powerful in this context is its ability to provide actionable insights based on its analysis. Rather than just identifying problems, it can suggest solutions. In the case of a bottleneck, it might recommend redistributing certain responsibilities among team members based on their current workload and areas of expertise. For addressing disconnects, it could suggest changes in communication channels or recommend team-building exercises designed to improve inclusivity and collaboration.

By providing these actionable insights, AI serves as a tool for continuous improvement within a team. It allows for a more nuanced understanding of team dynamics, which is crucial for effective decision-making. When communication flows smoothly and all team members are engaged, decisions are likely to be more well-rounded and take into account diverse perspectives. This not only improves the quality of the work but also contributes to a more positive and collaborative work environment.

The ability of AI to analyze communication patterns offers a transformative approach to improving team dynamics and decision-making. By identifying bottlenecks and disconnects proactively, and by offering actionable insights for addressing these issues, AI empowers teams to function more cohesively and make better decisions, ultimately contributing to more successful project outcomes.

Real-time Conflict Resolution

Artificial Intelligence is increasingly being recognized for its potential to monitor and analyze human interactions, including team communications within a project setting. One of the most promising applications of this capability is in conflict identification and resolution. Conflicts within a team, if not addressed promptly, can escalate into major issues that can derail a project. Traditional methods of identifying conflicts often rely on human observation and self-reporting, which can be subjective and may not capture conflicts until they have already escalated. AI offers a more proactive and objective approach.

By continuously monitoring team communications across various channels, such as emails, chat messages, and even transcribed voice meetings, AI algorithms can identify signs of potential conflicts before they become critical issues. These algorithms are designed to pick up on specific keywords, tone, and patterns of interaction that may indicate tension or disagreement among team members. For example, if the algorithm detects an increase in negative sentiment in communications between two team members, or if it identifies a pattern of one team member consistently overriding or dismissing the contributions of another, it can flag these as potential signs of conflict.

The real value of AI in this context lies in its ability to not just identify but also suggest strategies for resolving these conflicts. Based on the nature and severity of the conflict, the AI system can recommend different approaches for mediation. For minor conflicts that appear to be based on misunderstandings or lack of clear communication, the AI might suggest immediate actions such as clarifying project roles or objectives. In cases where the conflict appears to be more deep-seated, involving personality clashes or competition for resources, the AI could recommend more formal mediation strategies, such as involving a third-party mediator or escalating the issue to higher management.

These recommendations are not just based on the current conflict at hand but can also take into account historical data on what conflict resolution strategies have been effective within the team or organization in the past. This makes the recommendations more targeted and increases the likelihood of successful resolution. Moreover, by identifying and addressing conflicts early, the AI system helps to prevent the negative impact that unresolved conflicts can have on team morale and project outcomes. It allows for timely intervention, which is often crucial in conflict resolution, and frees up the project manager to focus on other aspects of project management that require human expertise.

In essence, AI's ability to monitor team communications for potential conflicts and suggest strategies for resolution represents a significant advancement in the field of project management. It offers a proactive, data-driven approach to conflict resolution, enabling teams to address issues before they escalate into major problems. This not only improves team dynamics but also contributes to more successful project outcomes, making it a valuable tool for any project manager.

Automating Administrative Tasks

Artificial Intelligence is making significant inroads into automating administrative tasks that, while essential, can consume a disproportionate amount of time and attention in a project setting. One area where AI's impact is particularly noticeable is in the management of meetings, a critical but often time-consuming aspect of project coordination. From scheduling and agenda-setting to the distribution of minutes, AI can handle these tasks with a level of efficiency and accuracy that frees team members to focus on more substantive work.

Scheduling meetings is often a complex task, especially for teams that are dispersed across different time zones or have varying work schedules. AI algorithms can analyze multiple calendars in real-time to find a time slot that is convenient for all participants. The algorithms take into account not just the availability but also the preferences of team members, such as their most productive hours or any recurring commitments they may have. This ensures that meetings are scheduled at a time when participants are most likely to be focused and engaged, thereby increasing the meeting's effectiveness.

Once a meeting time is set, the next task is to create an agenda that outlines the topics to be discussed and the objectives to be achieved. Here too, AI can offer valuable assistance. By analyzing previous meeting minutes, ongoing project tasks, and any flagged issues, AI can generate a draft agenda that covers all the critical points that need to be discussed. This draft can then be reviewed and fine-tuned by the project manager or team members, ensuring that the meeting stays focused and achieves its objectives. The AI can even prioritize agenda items based on their urgency or importance, helping to guide the flow of the meeting.

The final step in the meeting process is the distribution of minutes, which serves as a record of what was discussed and what decisions were made. This is another task that, while essential, can be time-consuming. AI can automate this process by transcribing the meeting, extracting key points, decisions, and action items, and then generating a set of minutes that can be distributed to all participants. Advanced Natural Language Processing algorithms ensure that the minutes are not just a verbatim transcript but a coherent summary that highlights the most important aspects of the meeting.

By automating these administrative tasks, AI allows team members to focus on the actual content of the meeting and the work that needs to be done to move the project forward. They can engage more deeply in discussions, contribute more effectively to decision-making, and spend more time on tasks that require their unique skills and expertise. This shift in focus from administrative tasks to substantive work can have a significant impact on both the efficiency and the quality of the project.

The integration of AI into the management of meetings represents a significant step forward in project management. By automating the scheduling, agenda-setting, and minute-distribution processes, AI not only improves the efficiency of meetings but also enhances their effectiveness by enabling team members to focus on what truly matters. This contributes to better decision-making, improved team dynamics, and ultimately, more successful project outcomes.

Section 4: Case Studies

Case Study 1: AI in Remote Team Management

Introduction

In today's increasingly remote work environment, effective communication and collaboration are more critical than ever. This case study explores how SoftDevCo, a mid-sized software development company, leveraged Artificial Intelligence (AI)-powered tools to enhance communication and collaboration among its remote team members. The result was a remarkable 30% increase in project efficiency, setting a new standard for what remote teams can achieve.

Background

SoftDevCo had been facing challenges in managing remote teams spread across multiple time zones. Communication gaps, misunderstandings, and delays were common, affecting the overall efficiency and morale of the team. Traditional project management tools were not sufficient to address these challenges, prompting the company to look for innovative solutions.

The Solution: AI-Powered Tools

After a comprehensive evaluation, SoftDevCo decided to implement an AI-powered project management and communication platform designed to enhance remote team collaboration. The platform offered a range of features, including real-time data analytics, intelligent task assignment, and automated meeting scheduling.

Real-Time Data Analytics

The platform continuously monitored various project metrics, such as task completion rates and team engagement levels. Whenever it detected an issue, like a task taking longer than expected, it would automatically flag it for immediate attention. This proactive approach helped the team address problems before they escalated, reducing delays and improving overall efficiency.

Intelligent Task Assignment

The platform used machine learning algorithms to analyze various factors like team members' skills, workload, and past performance. It then assigned tasks in a way that maximized efficiency, ensuring that each team member was working on tasks that aligned with their strengths and availability.

Automated Meeting Scheduling

Scheduling meetings across multiple time zones had always been a logistical nightmare for SoftDevCo. The AI-powered platform simplified this by analyzing team members' calendars and preferences to find the most convenient time slots, thereby increasing meeting attendance and engagement.

Results

After implementing the AI-powered platform, SoftDevCo experienced a significant improvement in various key performance indicators:

- A 30% increase in project efficiency
- A 25% reduction in communication-related delays
- A 20% improvement in team engagement and morale

Ethical Considerations

While the AI-powered platform was highly effective, it also raised questions about data privacy and surveillance. SoftDevCo addressed these concerns by implementing strict data privacy protocols and ensuring compliance with relevant regulations. Team members were also educated about the platform's capabilities and limitations, and their informed consent was obtained before implementation.

Conclusion

The implementation of AI-powered tools at SoftDevCo revolutionized the way the company managed its remote teams. By automating routine tasks and providing real-time insights, the platform allowed team members to focus on more substantive work, leading to a significant increase in project efficiency. However, the journey was not without challenges, particularly concerning ethical considerations around data privacy. By addressing these proactively, SoftDevCo was able to leverage the benefits of AI while also managing its risks responsibly, setting a new standard for remote team management in the software development industry.

Case Study 2: AI in Crisis Management

Introduction

Effective communication is the cornerstone of any emergency response operation, especially during natural disasters where every second counts. This case study delves into how an emergency response team leveraged Artificial Intelligence (AI) to optimize real-time communication during a catastrophic hurricane, leading to significantly improved response times and coordination among various units.

Background

The emergency response team faced the monumental task of coordinating rescue and relief operations during Hurricane Delta, a Category 5 storm that affected millions of people. Traditional communication systems were overwhelmed, leading to delays and miscommunications that could potentially cost lives. The team needed a solution that could handle the complexities of real-time decision-making in a high-stakes environment.

The Solution: AI-Powered Communication Platform

After a rapid evaluation process, the emergency response team implemented an AI-powered communication platform specifically designed for crisis situations. The platform had several key features:

Real-Time Data Analysis

The platform could analyze data from multiple sources in real-time, including weather forecasts, traffic conditions, and emergency calls. This enabled the command center to make data-driven decisions quickly.

Dynamic Resource Allocation

Using machine learning algorithms, the platform could predict where resources like ambulances, firefighters, and medical supplies would be needed the most. This allowed for proactive resource allocation, ensuring that help arrived where it was most urgently required.

Automated Alerts and Updates

The system was capable of sending automated alerts and updates to various units based on real-time conditions. For example, if a new area was identified as high-risk, nearby units would automatically receive notifications to proceed there.

Results

The impact of the AI-powered communication platform was immediate and profound:

Response times improved by 40%, as units received real-time data and could move more strategically. Coordination among different units, like fire, police, and medical teams, was significantly enhanced, leading to more effective joint operations.
The platform helped avoid resource wastage by accurately predicting where resources would be needed the most.

Ethical and Privacy Considerations

Given the sensitive nature of the data involved, the team took stringent measures to ensure data privacy and security. All data was encrypted, and strict access controls were implemented. The team also made sure to comply with all relevant laws and regulations concerning data use in emergency situations.

Conclusion

The use of an AI-powered communication platform revolutionized the emergency response team's ability to react to the rapidly changing conditions during Hurricane Delta. By optimizing real-time communication, the platform enabled quicker response times and better coordination among various units, undoubtedly saving lives and reducing property damage. While the technology was incredibly beneficial, it was used responsibly, with careful attention to ethical and privacy considerations. This case study serves as a compelling example of how AI can be leveraged for social good in critical, life-or-death situations.

Section 5: Tools and Platforms for AI-Enhanced Collaboration and Communication

Overview of Available Tools

The landscape of project management is undergoing a transformative shift with the advent of Artificial Intelligence. AI tools designed to enhance team collaboration and communication are at the forefront of this change, offering a range of features that promise to make project management more efficient and effective. These tools are not just incremental improvements on existing technologies but represent a paradigm shift in how teams collaborate and communicate.

One of the most prominent features of AI-powered collaboration tools is real-time data analysis. These tools can continuously monitor various project metrics, from task completion rates to team engagement levels, providing insights that can inform decision-making. For instance, if the tool detects that a particular task is taking longer than expected, it can automatically flag this issue, allowing the project manager to intervene before it becomes a significant problem. This proactive approach to problem-solving is a game-changer in project management, reducing the risk of delays and cost overruns.

Another groundbreaking feature is intelligent task assignment. Using machine learning algorithms, these tools can analyze a range of factors, such as team members' skills, workload, and past performance, to assign tasks in a way that maximizes efficiency and effectiveness. This goes beyond simple load balancing to create a truly optimized workflow, where each team member is assigned tasks that align with their strengths and availability.

Despite these advantages, AI-powered collaboration tools are not without their drawbacks. One of the main concerns is data privacy. These tools often require access to a wide range of data, from internal communications to individual performance metrics. While this data is essential for the tool's functionality, it also poses a risk if not properly secured. Companies need to be vigilant in ensuring that these tools comply with data protection regulations and that adequate cybersecurity measures are in place.

Another concern is the potential for algorithmic bias. If the machine learning algorithms that power these tools are trained on biased data, they can perpetuate or even exacerbate existing inequalities. For example, if a tool has been trained on data from a workplace where certain groups are underrepresented, it may replicate these biases in its task assignments, perpetuating a cycle of inequality. It's crucial for companies to be aware of this risk and to take steps to ensure that the algorithms are trained on diverse and representative data sets.

Cost is another factor that can be a barrier to adoption, especially for smaller organizations. While these tools promise long-term gains in efficiency and effectiveness, they often require a significant upfront investment. This includes not just the cost of the software itself but also the costs associated with training staff and integrating the tool into existing workflows. Companies need to weigh these costs against the potential benefits to determine if the investment is justified.

AI-powered tools designed to enhance team collaboration and communication offer a range of features that can significantly improve project management. From real-time data analysis to intelligent task assignment, these tools promise to make teams more efficient and effective. However, they also pose challenges in terms of data privacy, algorithmic bias, and cost. Companies considering adopting these tools need to be aware of both their pros and cons and take a holistic approach to ensure that they are implemented in a way that maximizes their benefits while mitigating their risks.

How to Choose the Right AI Tools

Selecting the right Artificial Intelligence tools for your team is a critical decision that can have a lasting impact on the efficiency and effectiveness of your projects. Given the plethora of options available, it's essential to consider various factors that go beyond just the immediate functionality of the tool. One of the most important considerations is scalability. As your team grows and the complexity of your projects increases, you'll need a tool that can grow with you. Scalability is not just about the ability to handle a larger volume of tasks or data but also about the tool's flexibility to adapt to changing workflows and project requirements. A scalable tool will allow you to add new features or modules as needed, ensuring that it remains relevant and useful as your needs evolve.

Ease of integration with existing systems is another crucial factor. Most organizations already have a range of software tools that they use for various aspects of project management, from data storage and communication to financial tracking. The AI tool you choose should be able to integrate seamlessly with these existing systems, both to streamline the workflow and to avoid the duplication of data. Poor integration can lead to inefficiencies, such as having to manually transfer data between systems, and increases the risk of errors. Therefore, it's essential to look for tools that offer robust integration options, either through built-in connectors for popular software or through customizable APIs that allow for more tailored integration.

Compliance with data privacy regulations is a concern that cannot be overlooked. AI tools often require access to sensitive data, from internal communications to individual performance metrics. The handling of this data must comply with all relevant privacy regulations, such as the General Data Protection Regulation (GDPR) in Europe or the California Consumer Privacy Act (CCPA) in the United States. Non-compliance can result in hefty fines and can also damage your organization's reputation. Therefore, it's essential to thoroughly vet any potential tool for its compliance with data privacy regulations. This includes not just the tool itself but also any third-party services it may use, such as cloud storage providers.

In addition to these primary factors, there are other considerations that, while perhaps not as critical, can still influence the success of the tool within your organization. These include the quality of customer support, the availability of training resources, and the tool's user interface and overall user experience. A tool that is difficult to use will face resistance from team members, reducing its effectiveness regardless of how powerful its features may be. On the other hand, a tool that offers a smooth user experience and robust support can facilitate quicker adoption and more effective use, maximizing the return on your investment.

Selecting an AI tool for your team is a complex decision that requires a multifaceted approach. Scalability, ease of integration with existing systems, and compliance with data privacy regulations are primary factors that need to be carefully considered. However, other aspects like customer support, training resources, and user experience can also play a significant role. By taking the time to evaluate each of these factors thoroughly, you can increase the likelihood of choosing a tool that not only meets your immediate needs but also offers long-term value for your organization.

Section 6: Ethical and Social Considerations

Data Privacy and Surveillance Concerns

The use of Artificial Intelligence to monitor team communications is a double-edged sword. On one hand, it offers unprecedented capabilities for improving team dynamics, identifying conflicts, and enhancing overall project management. On the other hand, it raises significant ethical questions around data privacy and surveillance. Striking the right balance between leveraging the benefits of AI and respecting individual privacy is a complex challenge that organizations must navigate carefully.

Data privacy is a primary concern when using AI to monitor team communications. While the intent may be to improve team collaboration, the fact remains that these tools have access to potentially sensitive information. This could range from personal conversations between team members to confidential project details. The collection and analysis of this data must be done in strict compliance with data privacy regulations, such as the General Data Protection Regulation (GDPR) in Europe or the California Consumer Privacy Act (CCPA) in the United States. However, compliance with legal requirements is just the minimum standard; organizations must also consider the ethical implications of this data collection.

Team members should be fully informed about what data is being collected, how it will be used, and what measures are in place to protect their privacy. Transparency is crucial in building trust and ensuring that the use of AI is seen as a tool for improvement rather than a form of surveillance.

The issue of surveillance is particularly thorny. The line between monitoring for performance improvement and outright surveillance can be thin, and it's easy to cross it inadvertently. Even if the data collected is not misused, the mere knowledge that one is being monitored can have a chilling effect on team members, stifling creativity and open communication. Therefore, it's essential to establish clear boundaries on what the AI tool will and will not monitor. For instance, while it may be acceptable to analyze communications related to project tasks for the purpose of improving efficiency, monitoring personal conversations between team members would likely be considered an invasion of privacy.

Managing these ethical considerations responsibly requires a multi-faceted approach. First and foremost, there should be a clear policy outlining the use of AI in monitoring team communications, including what data will be collected, how it will be used, and what measures are in place to protect privacy. This policy should be developed in consultation with legal, ethical, and data privacy experts to ensure that it meets all regulatory and ethical standards. Once the policy is in place, it's crucial to communicate it clearly to all team members and obtain their informed consent before implementing the AI tool. Ongoing education and training can help team members understand the benefits of the tool and how to use it responsibly, reducing the risk of misuse or misunderstanding.

The use of AI to monitor team communications offers significant benefits but also raises complex ethical questions around data privacy and surveillance. Organizations must navigate these challenges carefully, balancing the need for improved efficiency and collaboration with the imperative to respect individual privacy. This requires a comprehensive approach that includes compliance with data privacy regulations, transparent communication with team members, and ongoing education and training. By taking these steps, organizations can leverage the benefits of AI while also managing its ethical implications responsibly.

The Human Element

Artificial Intelligence has made remarkable strides in enhancing various aspects of project management, including communication. From automating administrative tasks like scheduling to providing real-time analytics that can guide decision-making, AI offers a range of tools that can make teams more efficient and effective. However, it's crucial to recognize that while AI can augment communication, it cannot replace the human element that is at the heart of effective teamwork. Empathy, understanding, and creative problem-solving are qualities that, at least for now, remain uniquely human and are essential for the success of any team.

Empathy is the ability to understand and share the feelings of others, and it plays a critical role in team dynamics. Team members who are empathetic are better able to understand the perspectives of their colleagues, leading to more effective communication and conflict resolution. While AI can flag potential conflicts based on the analysis of communication patterns, it cannot understand the emotional nuances behind these conflicts. It can tell you that a conflict exists, but it can't tell you why it exists or how to resolve it in a way that respects the emotional needs of all parties involved. That requires human intervention, guided by empathy and emotional intelligence.

Understanding is closely related to empathy but extends beyond it to include the comprehension of complex issues and concepts. In any project, there will be challenges that require a deep understanding of various factors, from technical specifications to market dynamics. AI can provide data that can inform this understanding, but it can't make the intuitive leaps that often lead to the most innovative solutions. For example, while AI can analyze customer behavior to guide product development, it can't understand why a particular feature resonates emotionally with customers. That level of understanding requires human insight, informed by a combination of data and emotional intelligence.

Creative problem-solving is another area where the human element is irreplaceable. While AI is excellent at analyzing data to identify problems and even suggest solutions, it is not capable of the kind of creative thinking that can lead to groundbreaking innovations. AI algorithms are designed to find the most efficient solution based on existing data, but they can't think outside the box to come up with entirely new approaches to a problem. This kind of creativity is essential in today's rapidly evolving business landscape, where the challenges teams face are often complex and unprecedented.

While AI offers powerful tools for enhancing communication and other aspects of project management, it is not a substitute for the human qualities that make effective teamwork possible. Empathy allows for more effective communication and conflict resolution, understanding enables the deep comprehension of complex challenges, and creative problem-solving leads to innovative solutions. As organizations increasingly adopt AI to improve efficiency, it's crucial to remember that these tools should be used to augment human abilities, not replace them. By leveraging the strengths of both AI and human intelligence, teams can be more effective than ever, achieving a level of performance that neither could reach on its own.

Conclusion: The Future of Team Collaboration and Communication

AI offers promising avenues for enhancing team collaboration and communication, making projects more efficient and effective. However, it's crucial to approach these technologies thoughtfully, considering both their potential benefits and ethical implications. As AI continues to evolve, project managers who successfully integrate these tools will be better positioned to lead teams to new heights of success.

CHAPTER 6: ETHICAL AND LEGAL IMPLICATIONS OF AI IN PROJECT MANAGEMENT

Introduction: The Double-Edged Sword of AI

While the previous chapters have focused on the transformative potential of AI in various aspects of project management, it's crucial to address the ethical and legal considerations that come with this technological revolution. AI is a double-edged sword; it offers immense benefits but also poses significant challenges that project managers must navigate responsibly. This chapter aims to provide a comprehensive overview of the ethical and legal landscape surrounding the use of AI in project management.

Section 1: Ethical Considerations in AI Deployment

Algorithmic Bias and Fairness

The promise of Artificial Intelligence in project management is immense, offering capabilities from automating mundane tasks to providing deep insights through data analytics. However, the technology is not without its pitfalls, one of the most concerning being the potential for AI algorithms to perpetuate or even exacerbate existing biases in society. This can lead to unfair or discriminatory outcomes that not only undermine the effectiveness of the project but also pose ethical and legal risks. Therefore, project managers have a critical role to play in ensuring that AI tools are designed and deployed in a manner that minimizes bias.

Bias in AI algorithms can manifest in various ways, often reflecting the prejudices present in the data on which they were trained. For example, if an AI tool used for recruitment has been trained on historical hiring data that reflects gender bias, the tool is likely to recommend male candidates over equally qualified female candidates. Similarly, an AI system used for performance evaluation could unfairly penalize certain groups if it has been trained on biased data. The implications are serious, affecting not just the individuals who are unfairly treated but also the overall integrity and success of the project.

Project managers must be vigilant from the outset, starting with the selection of the AI tool. Due diligence is required to ensure that the tool has been designed with bias minimization in mind. This could involve scrutinizing the training data to ensure it is representative and free from obvious biases, as well as evaluating the algorithm itself to check whether it includes mechanisms for bias detection and correction. Some advanced AI tools now come with built-in 'fairness' metrics that provide an empirical measure of the tool's propensity for bias, and opting for such tools could be a prudent choice.

Once a tool has been selected, ongoing monitoring is essential. Even if an AI tool starts off being relatively unbiased, it can develop biases over time as it continues to learn from new data. Regular audits can help detect any emerging biases, allowing for timely intervention. These audits should be conducted not just by technical experts but also by stakeholders who can provide diverse perspectives, including those related to ethics and social implications.

Training is another crucial aspect. Team members who will be using the AI tool need to be educated about the potential for bias and how to mitigate it. They should be trained to critically evaluate the recommendations or insights provided by the AI, rather than accepting them uncritically. This human oversight is an essential layer of defense against algorithmic bias, ensuring that decisions are fair and just.

In conclusion, while AI offers tremendous benefits for project management, it also poses risks in the form of algorithmic bias. Project managers have a responsibility to ensure that AI tools are designed and deployed in a way that minimizes this bias, through careful selection, ongoing monitoring, and training. By taking these steps, project managers can harness the power of AI while also upholding the ethical standards that are crucial for the success and integrity of the project.

Strategies for Mitigating Bias

Ensuring that the data used to train Artificial Intelligence algorithms is representative of diverse perspectives is a critical step in minimizing bias and enhancing the fairness of AI systems. The quality and diversity of training data have a direct impact on the performance of AI algorithms, shaping not just how well the algorithm performs but also how equitable its decisions are. When the training data is skewed or unrepresentative, the AI system is more likely to produce biased or unfair outcomes, which can have serious ethical and legal implications.

The importance of diverse training data is evident across various applications of AI, from natural language processing and image recognition to more complex tasks like predictive analytics in healthcare or finance. For instance, if a facial recognition system is trained primarily on images of people from a particular ethnic background, it is likely to perform poorly—and more problematically, unfairly—when applied to people from other ethnic backgrounds. Similarly, a healthcare predictive model trained on data from a specific demographic may not accurately predict disease outcomes for individuals outside of that demographic.

To ensure diversity in training data, it's essential to include a wide range of variables that capture different perspectives and experiences. This could mean incorporating data from various geographical locations, age groups, gender identities, and cultural backgrounds. In more technical terms, the dataset should span the full feature space of the problem being addressed, so that the algorithm learns to make decisions based on a comprehensive understanding of diverse conditions and scenarios.

However, merely having diverse data is not enough; it's also crucial to handle the data responsibly to ensure that it is used ethically and does not reinforce existing inequalities. This involves careful data curation and preprocessing to identify and mitigate any biases in the data. For example, if a dataset contains a disproportionate number of negative outcomes for a particular group, weighting techniques can be used to balance the dataset and mitigate the risk of bias. Additionally, ethical considerations may require that certain types of sensitive data, such as those related to race or religion, be handled with extra care to prevent discriminatory outcomes.

Transparency is another key aspect of using diverse training data responsibly. Stakeholders, including those who use the AI system and those who are affected by its decisions, should be informed about how the data was collected, what it includes, and how it was used to train the algorithm. This transparency can build trust and provide an opportunity for stakeholders to identify potential issues that may not have been apparent to the developers of the AI system.

Ensuring that the data used to train AI algorithms is representative of diverse perspectives is a complex but crucial task. It involves not just collecting diverse data but also handling it responsibly and transparently. By doing so, we can develop AI systems that are not only high-performing but also fair and equitable, thereby realizing the full potential of AI to benefit a wide range of people.

Regularly reviewing algorithms to identify and rectify any biases is an essential practice for ensuring the ethical and fair deployment of Artificial Intelligence. As AI systems increasingly influence various aspects of our lives, from employment and healthcare to criminal justice and finance, the importance of algorithmic fairness cannot be overstated. Algorithm audits serve as a mechanism to scrutinize the decision-making processes of these systems, providing an opportunity to detect, understand, and correct biases that may have inadvertently been introduced.

The need for algorithm audits stems from the fact that biases can enter AI systems in numerous ways. They can be present in the training data, as discussed earlier, or they can be a result of the algorithmic design itself. Even well-intentioned efforts to create fair algorithms can fall short due to the complexities of human bias and the limitations of mathematical models to capture these nuances. Furthermore, as algorithms continue to learn and adapt over time, new biases can emerge, making ongoing audits crucial.

The process of conducting an algorithm audit involves several steps. The first is defining what fairness means in the context of the specific AI application. Different situations may require different fairness metrics; for example, fairness in a healthcare algorithm might involve ensuring equal predictive accuracy across different demographic groups, while fairness in a hiring algorithm might focus on ensuring that the selection process is not influenced by gender or ethnicity. Once the fairness metrics are defined, the next step is to evaluate the algorithm against these metrics using a variety of testing methods, which could range from statistical tests to user experience studies.

If biases are detected during the audit, the next step is to understand their source. This could involve a detailed analysis of the training data, the algorithm's decision-making process, or both. Understanding the source of bias is crucial for devising effective strategies to rectify it. These strategies could involve re-balancing the training data, modifying the algorithmic design, or even redefining the fairness metrics if they are found to be inadequate.

It's important to note that algorithm audits are not a one-time activity but rather an ongoing process. As algorithms evolve and as societal norms and values change, the definition of what is considered fair can also change. Regular audits ensure that the algorithm continues to meet the fairness criteria, even as it adapts to new data and conditions.

Transparency and accountability are also key aspects of algorithm audits. The findings of the audit, including any biases that were detected and the steps taken to rectify them, should be communicated clearly to all stakeholders. This not only builds trust but also opens the door for external audits and peer reviews, which can provide additional perspectives and insights.

Algorithm audits are a critical tool for ensuring that AI systems are deployed in a manner that is both ethical and fair. By regularly reviewing algorithms to identify and rectify biases, we can mitigate the risks associated with the increasing influence of AI in decision-making processes. This practice is essential for realizing the full potential of AI as a force for good, benefiting a wide range of individuals and communities.

Data Privacy and Consent

The use of Artificial Intelligence in project management is often synonymous with the collection and analysis of large volumes of data. This data can range from project timelines and resource allocation metrics to more sensitive information like employee performance reviews or customer feedback. In some instances, the data may even include personal identifiers or other sensitive attributes that could be subject to privacy concerns. Given this landscape, project managers have a pivotal role in ensuring that data is handled responsibly and that proper consent is obtained where necessary.

The first layer of responsibility involves understanding the types of data that are being collected and for what purpose. Project managers should work closely with data scientists and legal advisors to categorize the data and assess the associated risks and compliance requirements. For example, if the project involves analyzing customer behavior, it's crucial to understand whether the data can be anonymized or if it contains personally identifiable information that would subject it to privacy laws such as the General Data Protection Regulation (GDPR) in Europe or the California Consumer Privacy Act (CCPA) in the United States.

Once the nature of the data is understood, the next step is to ensure that it is collected and stored in a secure manner. This involves implementing robust cybersecurity measures to protect against unauthorized access or data breaches. Data encryption, secure data transfer protocols, and stringent access controls are some of the methods that can be employed to safeguard data. Additionally, data should be stored in a way that facilitates compliance with data retention policies, which may require that data be deleted after a certain period or once it has served its intended purpose.

Obtaining proper consent is another critical aspect of responsible data handling. If the data includes personal or sensitive information, informed consent must be obtained from the individuals to whom the data pertains. This consent process should be transparent, providing clear information about what data is being collected, how it will be used, and how long it will be retained. In some cases, such as when dealing with minors or other vulnerable populations, additional safeguards may be required to ensure that consent is freely given and fully informed.

Even after data has been collected, the responsibility for its ethical use continues. Project managers should oversee how the data is analyzed and applied, ensuring that it is used in a manner consistent with the consent provided and that it does not lead to unfair or discriminatory outcomes. This is particularly important when using AI algorithms that may have the potential to amplify existing biases in the data or introduce new biases through their decision-making processes.

The use of AI in project management brings with it the responsibility to handle data in an ethical and compliant manner. From understanding the types of data being collected to implementing secure storage measures and obtaining proper consent, project managers play a crucial role in ensuring that data is handled responsibly. This not only mitigates legal and ethical risks but also builds trust among stakeholders, thereby enhancing the overall credibility and success of the project.

Data Protection Regulations

GDPR: The General Data Protection Regulation in the European Union.

CCPA: The California Consumer Privacy Act in the United States.

Section 2: Legal Implications of AI in Project Management

Intellectual Property Rights

As Artificial Intelligence systems continue to evolve and become more sophisticated, they are increasingly capable of producing outputs that, in a traditional context, would be considered the intellectual property of a human creator. These outputs can range from written articles and music compositions to software code and even scientific discoveries. The question of who owns these outputs is a complex and evolving legal and ethical issue that challenges our traditional understanding of intellectual property rights.

Traditionally, intellectual property rights, including copyrights and patents, are granted to human creators to incentivize innovation and creativity. These rights provide creators with exclusive control over their creations, allowing them to benefit financially from their work. However, as AI systems begin to produce work that resembles human creativity, the lines become blurred. Can a machine be considered a "creator" in the legal sense? And if not, who owns the rights to the work it produces?

One perspective argues that the ownership of AI-generated outputs should belong to the human operators of the AI system, such as the developers or the entity that commissioned the work. This viewpoint is rooted in the idea that although the AI system may have generated the output, it was created using algorithms and data that were provided by humans. The AI system itself lacks the ability to have intentions or make creative choices; it operates based on the parameters set by its human operators. Therefore, the intellectual effort behind the AI-generated output can be attributed to the humans who designed, trained, and operated the AI system.

However, this perspective becomes more complicated as AI systems advance to the point where they can learn and adapt autonomously, making decisions that were not explicitly programmed by their human operators. In such cases, attributing the intellectual effort solely to the human creators becomes less straightforward. Some have proposed that a new category of intellectual property rights should be created to account for AI-generated outputs, which could involve shared ownership between human operators and the AI entity itself, although this raises further questions about the legal status of AI systems.

Another layer of complexity is added when considering the data used to train the AI system. If the AI system was trained using publicly available data or data contributed by multiple parties, determining ownership becomes even more challenging. Could the contributors of the data claim some rights to the AI-generated output? And what happens if the AI system was trained on data that was obtained unethically or without proper consent?

Ethical considerations also come into play. For instance, if an AI system generates a piece of work that has significant social, cultural, or scientific value, some argue that it should be considered a public good, with ownership rights held collectively rather than by a single entity.

The question of who owns the outputs generated by sophisticated AI systems is a complex issue that challenges our traditional understanding of intellectual property rights. As AI continues to advance, it will be essential for legal systems to evolve in tandem to address these challenges. This will likely involve a multidisciplinary approach, incorporating insights from law, ethics, and technology to develop a framework that is both fair and adaptable to future advancements in AI.

Liability and Accountability

The question of accountability when an Artificial Intelligence system makes a decision with legal or financial ramifications is a pressing concern in today's rapidly evolving technological landscape. As AI systems are increasingly integrated into various sectors like healthcare, finance, and legal services, the decisions they make can have profound impacts on individuals and organizations alike. These impacts can range from financial losses and legal disputes to more severe outcomes like health complications or even loss of life in extreme cases. Given these stakes, determining accountability is both a legal and ethical imperative.

Traditionally, accountability in decision-making processes is straightforward: it rests with the human individuals or entities that make the decisions. However, the introduction of AI complicates this framework. AI systems can analyze vast amounts of data and make decisions or recommendations based on complex algorithms that even their developers may not fully understand due to the "black box" nature of some machine learning models. So, when an AI system makes a decision that leads to legal or financial repercussions, who is held accountable?

One perspective posits that the accountability should lie with the organization that deployed the AI system. This viewpoint is grounded in the principle of "vicarious liability," where an employer is responsible for the actions of its employees (or, in this case, its machines) performed in the course of employment. The organization, having made the decision to integrate AI into its operations, assumes the risks and responsibilities associated with the technology. This approach aligns with traditional business practices where the organization is accountable for its operational outcomes, whether they result from human or machine actions.

However, holding the organization solely accountable may not always be fair or effective in promoting responsible AI use. What about the role of the project manager who oversees the deployment of the AI system, or the developers who created the algorithms? They have a direct influence on how the AI system functions and, consequently, on the decisions it makes. Some argue that these individuals should share in the accountability. The project manager, for example, may be responsible for ensuring that the AI system is used ethically and that adequate safeguards are in place to prevent erroneous or biased decisions. Similarly, the developers could be held accountable if the algorithms they created are flawed or if they failed to adequately test the system for potential issues.

Another layer of complexity arises when multiple organizations or entities are involved. For instance, what happens if the AI system was developed by one company but deployed by another? Or what if the data used to train the system was provided by a third party? In such cases, accountability may be distributed among multiple stakeholders, requiring a more nuanced legal framework to apportion responsibility.

Ethical considerations also play a significant role in this discussion. The principle of "explainability" in AI ethics argues for transparent decision-making processes, especially when the decisions have significant ramifications. If an AI system's decision leads to legal or financial consequences, the affected parties have a right to understand how the decision was made, which further complicates the issue of accountability.

The question of who is held accountable when an AI system makes a decision with legal or financial implications is far from straightforward. It's a complex issue that intersects with legal doctrines, ethical principles, and the technical nuances of AI technology. As AI systems become more integrated into critical decision-making processes, there is an urgent need for a multidisciplinary approach to develop a robust framework for accountability that is both fair and adaptable to the evolving capabilities of AI.

Case Law Examples

AI in Healthcare: Legal cases where AI systems made incorrect diagnoses.

Introduction

Artificial Intelligence (AI) has been hailed as a revolutionary force in healthcare, promising to improve diagnostic accuracy, streamline administrative tasks, and even predict patient outcomes. However, the technology is not without its pitfalls. This case study explores legal cases where AI systems made incorrect diagnoses, leading to adverse patient outcomes and raising questions about accountability, ethics, and the limitations of AI in healthcare.

Background

AI systems in healthcare are often designed to assist or augment the capabilities of medical professionals. They analyze medical images, patient histories, and other data to provide diagnostic recommendations. While these systems have shown promise in improving diagnostic accuracy in many instances, there have been notable cases where they have failed, sometimes with dire consequences.

Case Examples

Case 1: Missed Cancer Diagnosis

In this case, an AI system designed to identify early signs of lung cancer failed to detect a malignant tumor in a 45-year-old patient. The patient was given an all-clear, leading to a delay in treatment and the eventual spread of cancer. A lawsuit was filed against the healthcare provider and the AI system's manufacturer, claiming negligence and lack of adequate testing.

Case 2: Incorrect Medication Prescription

An AI system designed to assist in medication management incorrectly diagnosed a patient's symptoms as indicative of a condition that required a specific medication. The patient suffered severe side effects from the medication, leading to hospitalization. Legal action was taken against the healthcare facility for relying solely on AI for diagnosis and treatment recommendations.

Case 3: False Positive in Cardiac Conditions

A renowned cardiac center used an AI system to analyze echocardiograms. The system incorrectly identified a healthy patient as being at high risk for a cardiac event. The patient underwent unnecessary surgical procedures and suffered both physical and emotional trauma. The patient sued the healthcare provider and the developers of the AI system for malpractice and emotional distress.

Legal and Ethical Implications

These cases raise several legal and ethical questions:

- Accountability: Who is held responsible when an AI system makes an incorrect diagnosis? Is it the healthcare provider, the AI developer, or both?
- Informed Consent: Were patients adequately informed that an AI system would be involved in their diagnosis and treatment? Did they consent to this?
- Transparency and Explainability: Are healthcare providers obligated to explain the role of AI in medical decision-making processes, especially when the AI system's decision-making is not transparent?
- Regulatory Oversight: Is there sufficient regulation governing the use of AI in healthcare, especially concerning testing and validation before these systems are deployed in a clinical setting?

Conclusions and Recommendations

The incorrect diagnoses made by AI systems in these cases had severe consequences, ranging from delayed or incorrect treatment to unnecessary surgical procedures. These incidents serve as cautionary tales for the healthcare industry, AI developers, and regulatory bodies.

- Robust Testing: AI systems must undergo rigorous testing for accuracy and reliability before being deployed in healthcare settings.
- Human Oversight: A medical professional should always review AI-generated diagnoses. Reliance solely on AI is not only risky but could also be considered negligent.
- Transparency: Patients must be informed when AI systems are involved in their healthcare and should have the option to consent or decline.
- Regulatory Framework: There is an urgent need for a comprehensive regulatory framework that addresses the ethical and legal challenges posed by the use of AI in healthcare.

While AI has the potential to revolutionize healthcare, its limitations and the ethical and legal challenges it presents cannot be ignored. Stakeholders must collaborate to address these challenges, ensuring that AI is deployed responsibly and effectively in healthcare settings.

AI in Finance: Instances where algorithmic trading led to significant financial losses.

Section 3: Social and Cultural Implications

Job Displacement and the Future of Work

The advent of Artificial Intelligence in various sectors has opened up unprecedented possibilities for automating tasks, optimizing processes, and even making complex decisions based on data analytics. While these advancements promise significant benefits, such as increased efficiency and cost savings, they also raise concerns about job displacement. As AI systems become capable of performing tasks that were traditionally the domain of human workers, the fear of widespread unemployment looms large. For project managers who are often at the forefront of implementing new technologies within an organization, the challenge is to leverage the benefits of AI while also mitigating concerns about job loss.

One way to approach this challenge is by adopting a strategy of augmentation rather than replacement. Instead of viewing AI as a technology that replaces human workers, it can be seen as a tool that enhances human capabilities and frees up workers to focus on more complex and creative tasks. For instance, in a customer service setting, AI chatbots can handle routine queries, allowing human agents to focus on more complicated issues that require emotional intelligence and nuanced understanding. By positioning AI as a complementary technology, project managers can help alleviate fears of job displacement.

Education and retraining programs are another crucial element in this equation. As AI systems take on more of the routine, manual tasks, the skill sets valued in the job market will likely shift. Project managers can play a proactive role in identifying these shifts and preparing their teams accordingly. This could involve offering training programs in areas like data analysis, machine learning, or other specialized skills that will be in high demand as AI adoption increases. By equipping team members with the skills they need to work alongside AI systems, project managers can help ensure a smoother transition and provide avenues for career growth.

Communication is also key to mitigating concerns about job displacement due to AI. Project managers should maintain an open dialogue with team members about the organization's AI strategy and how it will impact their roles. This includes being transparent about the timeline for AI implementation and what changes team members can expect in their day-to-day responsibilities. Providing a clear roadmap can help alleviate uncertainty and give employees a sense of control over their professional future.

Ethical considerations should also be part of the conversation. As stewards of project goals and organizational values, project managers have a responsibility to ensure that the adoption of AI is aligned with ethical principles, including fairness and transparency. This could involve conducting impact assessments to understand how AI implementation will affect not just jobs but also data privacy and security. Ethical AI use should be a cornerstone of any project that involves the technology.

The potential for job displacement due to AI is a legitimate concern that project managers must address as they integrate this technology into their operations. By adopting a strategy that focuses on augmentation rather than replacement, investing in education and retraining, maintaining open communication, and upholding ethical standards, project managers can help mitigate these concerns. This balanced approach allows organizations to leverage the undeniable benefits of AI while also preparing their human workforce for the changes that this transformative technology brings.

Ethical Considerations in Global Projects

Managing projects that span multiple countries is inherently complex, but when those projects involve the use of Artificial Intelligence, the complexity escalates significantly. Each country involved may have its own set of laws, regulations, and cultural norms concerning data privacy and the ethical use of AI. This creates a multifaceted ethical landscape that project managers must navigate with great care.

One of the most pressing issues in such scenarios is data privacy. Different countries have varying degrees of stringency when it comes to data protection laws. For instance, the European Union's General Data Protection Regulation (GDPR) is one of the most comprehensive data protection laws in the world, requiring explicit consent for data collection and providing individuals with extensive rights over their data. On the other hand, some countries may have lax or even non-existent data protection laws. Project managers must be well-versed in the legal requirements of each jurisdiction involved in the project to ensure that data is collected, stored, and processed in a manner that is compliant with local laws.

Cultural norms also play a significant role in shaping attitudes toward data privacy and AI. In some cultures, there may be a high level of trust in technology and a willingness to share personal information. In others, historical or societal factors may have led to a more skeptical or cautious approach to data sharing. Understanding these cultural nuances is crucial for project managers as they design and implement AI systems. For example, the way in which user consent is obtained for data collection may need to be adapted to fit the cultural context, going beyond mere legal compliance to also consider local customs and expectations.

The ethical use of AI is another area where laws and cultural norms can vary widely between countries. Ethical considerations such as algorithmic bias, transparency, and accountability may be viewed differently depending on the legal and cultural landscape. In some countries, there may be a strong emphasis on ensuring that AI systems are designed to be equitable and that they do not perpetuate existing social inequalities. In others, the focus may be more on innovation and economic competitiveness, with less attention paid to ethical considerations. Project managers must strive to find a balance that respects both the local context and universal principles of ethical AI use.

Navigating this complex ethical landscape requires a multifaceted approach. Legal expertise is essential to understand the regulatory requirements of each country involved in the project. Cultural sensitivity and local knowledge are also crucial for adapting project strategies to fit the local context. Ethical expertise, possibly in the form of ethical review boards or consultants, can provide valuable insights into how to navigate the often murky waters of AI ethics in a multinational context.

Managing AI projects that involve multiple countries is a complex task that requires careful consideration of both legal and cultural factors. By investing in legal, cultural, and ethical expertise, project managers can navigate this complexity and ensure that the project not only complies with local laws but also respects the cultural and ethical norms of each country involved. This not only mitigates risk but also contributes to the long-term success and sustainability of the project.

Section 4: Case Studies

Case Study 1: Ethical AI in Government Projects

Introduction
The implementation of Artificial Intelligence (AI) in public services has the potential to revolutionize how government agencies operate, promising increased efficiency, reduced costs, and improved outcomes. However, the stakes are particularly high when AI is applied to sensitive areas like social welfare allocation. This case study provides an in-depth look at how a government agency successfully implemented an AI system for social welfare allocation while carefully navigating the ethical and legal pitfalls that come with such a venture.

Background
The government agency in question oversees the allocation of social welfare benefits, a task that involves assessing individual needs, verifying eligibility, and distributing resources. Given the volume of applications and the complexity of the assessment process, the agency sought to leverage AI to

streamline operations. The primary objectives were to make the allocation process more efficient, reduce human error, and ensure that resources were distributed equitably.

The AI System

The AI system was designed to analyze a wide range of data, including income, employment history, health records, and more, to assess eligibility and determine the level of benefits for each applicant. Advanced machine learning algorithms were used to predict individual needs and allocate resources accordingly. The system was also designed to adapt and learn from its decisions, continually refining its algorithms to improve accuracy over time.

Ethical and Legal Challenges

The agency faced several ethical and legal challenges in implementing the AI system:

- Data Privacy: The system required access to sensitive personal data, raising concerns about data protection and privacy.
- Algorithmic Bias: Given that the system would be making decisions affecting vulnerable populations, there was a significant risk of algorithmic bias, which could lead to unfair or discriminatory outcomes.
- Transparency and Accountability: The "black box" nature of some machine learning algorithms could make it difficult to explain decisions, posing challenges for transparency and accountability.
- Legal Compliance: The agency had to ensure that the AI system complied with existing laws and regulations governing social welfare allocation, which varied significantly by jurisdiction.

Navigating the Pitfalls

Data Privacy

To address data privacy concerns, the agency worked closely with legal experts to ensure compliance with data protection laws. All data was anonymized and encrypted, and strict access controls were implemented. The agency also made it a point to obtain informed consent from all applicants, clearly explaining how their data would be used.

Algorithmic Bias

To mitigate the risk of algorithmic bias, the agency collaborated with third-party experts to conduct a thorough audit of the AI algorithms. The system was trained on a diverse dataset, and ongoing monitoring was put in place to identify and correct any biased outcomes.

Transparency and Accountability

The agency implemented a "human-in-the-loop" approach to ensure transparency and accountability. While the AI system provided recommendations, final decisions were made by human caseworkers who could review the AI's reasoning. An appeals process was also established for applicants who felt they had been treated unfairly.

Legal Compliance

To ensure legal compliance, the agency conducted a comprehensive review of relevant laws and regulations across all jurisdictions. The AI system was designed to be flexible, allowing for easy adjustments to algorithms and decision-making processes to comply with changing legal landscapes.

Outcomes and Lessons Learned

The AI system was successfully implemented and led to a significant increase in the efficiency of social welfare allocation. Application processing times were reduced by 30%, and the accuracy of allocations improved, leading to better outcomes for beneficiaries. However, the agency also learned valuable lessons about the importance of ongoing monitoring and the need for human oversight to ensure ethical and legal compliance.

Conclusion

The implementation of an AI system in social welfare allocation by a government agency demonstrated that it is possible to leverage the benefits of AI while carefully navigating ethical and legal pitfalls. By taking a proactive approach to address data privacy, algorithmic bias, transparency, and legal compliance, the agency was able to implement a system that not only improved efficiency but also upheld the ethical and legal standards expected in the sensitive area of social welfare.

Case Study 2: AI Ethics in a Multinational Corporation

Introduction

Artificial Intelligence (AI) is transforming the way businesses operate, offering unprecedented opportunities for innovation, efficiency, and competitive advantage. However, the rapid adoption of AI also raises complex ethical and legal questions that organizations must address. This case study explores how a multinational corporation developed an internal ethical framework for the deployment of AI across its global projects, navigating a landscape fraught with cultural, legal, and ethical complexities.

Background

The corporation in focus is a global leader in technology solutions, with operations spanning multiple continents and diverse markets. Recognizing the transformative potential of AI, the company sought to integrate machine learning, data analytics, and other AI technologies into its product offerings and internal processes. However, the multinational nature of the corporation added layers of complexity, as different countries have varying regulations and cultural norms concerning data privacy, algorithmic fairness, and other ethical considerations.

The Need for an Ethical Framework

The corporation identified several key areas where ethical considerations were paramount:

- Data Privacy and Security: Handling sensitive customer and employee data across different jurisdictions.
- Algorithmic Fairness: Ensuring that AI algorithms do not perpetuate existing biases or create unfair or discriminatory outcomes.
- Transparency and Accountability: Making the AI decision-making process understandable to stakeholders and establishing accountability mechanisms.
- Compliance and Governance: Adhering to the legal requirements of different countries while maintaining a consistent ethical stance.

Developing the Ethical Framework
Cross-Functional Team

The corporation assembled a cross-functional team comprising legal experts, ethicists, data scientists, and business leaders to develop the ethical framework. This diversity ensured that the framework would be comprehensive, balancing technical feasibility with ethical considerations and business objectives.

Stakeholder Consultation

The team conducted a series of consultations with internal and external stakeholders, including employees, customers, and regulatory bodies. These consultations provided valuable insights into the ethical concerns and expectations of different groups and helped shape the framework's guiding principles.

Guiding Principles

Based on their research and consultations, the team established a set of guiding principles for ethical AI deployment, which included respect for human rights, fairness, transparency, and accountability. These principles served as the foundation upon which the ethical framework was built.

Implementation Guidelines

The team developed specific implementation guidelines for each guiding principle, tailored to different business units and geographical locations. These guidelines provided practical steps for integrating ethical considerations into the AI development and deployment process.

Compliance Mechanisms

To ensure adherence to the framework, the team established a set of compliance mechanisms, including regular audits, reporting requirements, and a whistleblowing hotline for ethical concerns related to AI.

Outcomes and Impact

The ethical framework was rolled out company-wide through a series of training programs, workshops, and internal communications. Since its implementation, the corporation has seen several positive outcomes:

- Increased Trust: Both employees and customers reported increased trust in the company's use of AI, bolstering its reputation as an ethical leader in the technology industry.
- Regulatory Compliance: The framework facilitated compliance with varying international regulations, reducing legal risks and strengthening the company's position in global markets.
- Ethical Decision-Making: The framework has been instrumental in guiding ethical decision-making in AI projects, leading to more responsible and fair outcomes.
- Competitive Advantage: The ethical stance has become a differentiator in the market, attracting customers and partners who value responsible AI use.

Lessons Learned and Future Directions

The development and implementation of the ethical framework were not without challenges, including initial resistance from some business units and the complexity of adapting the framework to different cultural and legal contexts. However, the corporation learned that proactive engagement with ethical considerations is not just a compliance requirement but a business imperative.

The corporation plans to regularly update the framework to adapt to emerging ethical challenges and to conduct ongoing training to ensure that ethical considerations remain at the forefront of its AI initiatives.

Conclusion

The case study demonstrates that it is possible for multinational corporations to navigate the complex ethical landscape associated with AI. By taking a proactive, principle-based approach, the corporation was able to develop an ethical framework that has not only mitigated risks but also added value to the business. The experience offers valuable insights for other organizations seeking to responsibly harness the power of AI in a global context.

Section 5: Developing an Ethical Framework for AI in Project Management

Key Components of an Ethical Framework

Transparency: Clear documentation of how AI algorithms make decisions.

Accountability: Established lines of responsibility for AI decisions.

Inclusivity: Ensuring that AI systems are accessible and fair to all users.

Tools and Resources for Ethical AI

A review of existing guidelines, toolkits, and best practices for implementing ethical AI in project management.

Conclusion: The Ethical Imperative in AI-Driven Project Management

As AI becomes an integral part of project management, the ethical and legal considerations surrounding its use will become increasingly important. Project managers have a responsibility to navigate this complex landscape thoughtfully and responsibly. By doing so, they can not only mitigate risks but also contribute to the development of AI technologies that are ethical, fair, and beneficial for all.

CHAPTER 7: THE FUTURE OF AI IN PROJECT MANAGEMENT: TRENDS, OPPORTUNITIES, AND CHALLENGES

Introduction: The Ever-Evolving Landscape of AI

As we've explored in the preceding chapters, AI has already made significant inroads into the field of project management. However, the landscape of AI is ever-evolving, with new technologies, methodologies, and ethical considerations emerging regularly. This chapter aims to look ahead, exploring the future trends in AI that could impact project management, the opportunities these trends present, and the challenges that project managers will need to navigate.

Section 1: Emerging Trends in AI Technology

Quantum Computing and AI

The advent of quantum computing represents a paradigm shift in the realm of computational power, promising to bring transformative changes to various fields, including Artificial Intelligence (AI). Traditional computers use bits as the basic unit of information, which can be either a 0 or a 1. Quantum computers, on the other hand, use quantum bits or qubits, which can exist in multiple states simultaneously thanks to the principles of quantum mechanics. This fundamental difference allows quantum computers to perform complex calculations exponentially faster than their classical counterparts, opening up new horizons for AI algorithms that could become more efficient, more accurate, and more capable than ever before.

The potential impact of quantum computing on AI is vast and multi-dimensional. One of the most immediate benefits is speed. Many AI algorithms, particularly in the realm of machine learning, require the processing of enormous datasets to train models effectively. Classical computers can take days, weeks, or even months to complete these calculations. Quantum computers, with their ability to perform multiple calculations simultaneously, could reduce this time to hours or even minutes. This speedup could be particularly beneficial in fields like drug discovery or climate modeling, where time is of the essence.

Another area where quantum computing could revolutionize AI is optimization problems, which are pervasive in various applications of AI, from logistics and supply chain management to financial modeling. Classical computing methods often use heuristic approaches to find "good enough" solutions because finding the optimal solution would be too time-consuming. Quantum computing, with its ability to explore multiple solutions simultaneously, could find the true optimal solution in a fraction of the time, leading to more efficient and effective outcomes.

Quantum computing also holds promise for enhancing machine learning algorithms in more fundamental ways. For example, quantum versions of machine learning algorithms could identify complex patterns in data that classical algorithms might miss. This capability could be transformative in fields like healthcare, where subtle patterns in medical data could provide early indicators of diseases, or in cybersecurity, where identifying unusual patterns of network behavior could flag a potential security threat.

However, the integration of quantum computing and AI also presents significant challenges. Quantum computers are still in the experimental stage, and building a stable, scalable quantum computing system is a monumental scientific and engineering challenge. There are also issues related to quantum error correction, as quantum systems are highly susceptible to errors due to environmental factors like temperature and electromagnetic radiation.

Moreover, the development of quantum algorithms suitable for AI applications is an emerging field that requires a deep understanding of both quantum mechanics and machine learning principles. There's also the question of interpretability; as AI algorithms become more powerful and complex thanks to quantum computing, making these algorithms transparent and understandable becomes even more challenging.

Ethical and security considerations also come into play. The power of quantum computing could potentially break current encryption methods, posing risks to data privacy and security. As AI systems become more capable and make more significant decisions affecting human lives, ensuring these systems are ethical, fair, and secure becomes increasingly critical.

Quantum computing has the potential to revolutionize the computational power available for AI algorithms, making them exponentially faster and more efficient. This leap in computational capabilities could lead to breakthroughs in various fields, from healthcare and climate science to logistics and cybersecurity. However, realizing this potential requires overcoming significant scientific, engineering, and ethical challenges. As researchers and practitioners continue to explore the synergies between quantum computing and AI, the prospects for transformative change in how we understand and interact with the world become increasingly tangible.

Explainable AI (XAI)

The increasing complexity of Artificial Intelligence (AI) systems has led to remarkable advancements in various fields, from healthcare and finance to transportation and project management. These systems can analyze vast amounts of data, identify patterns, and make decisions with a level of speed and accuracy that often surpasses human capabilities. However, this complexity also presents a significant challenge: the "black box" problem, where the decision-making processes of AI algorithms are opaque and difficult to understand. As AI systems become more deeply integrated into critical aspects of our lives and businesses, the need for transparency and explainability has never been greater. This is where Explainable AI (XAI) comes into play, aiming to make the decision-making processes of AI algorithms understandable to humans.

The importance of XAI is multifaceted and extends across various sectors and applications. For instance, in healthcare, if an AI algorithm recommends a particular treatment for a patient, doctors need to understand the rationale behind that recommendation to trust it and to explain it to the patient. Similarly, in project management, if an AI system suggests reallocating resources or changing project timelines, project managers need to understand the reasoning behind these suggestions to make informed decisions and to justify those decisions to stakeholders.

XAI seeks to address these challenges by developing techniques that make the internal workings of AI models more transparent. One approach is to design algorithms that can provide "feature importance" scores, indicating which variables or data points were most influential in reaching a particular decision. For example, if an AI system is used to assess credit risk, an explainable model could indicate which factors—such as income level, employment history, or past spending behavior—were most influential in determining a person's creditworthiness.

Another approach in XAI is the use of "local interpretable model-agnostic explanations" (LIME), which approximates complex models with simpler, more interpretable models for individual predictions. In essence, LIME helps to explain the behavior of any classifier in a way that humans can understand, providing insights into what the model is "thinking."

The development of natural language interfaces for AI systems is also a significant step toward explainability. These interfaces can translate the complex mathematical computations of AI algorithms into human-readable explanations. For example, instead of merely stating that a patient has a 70% likelihood of having a particular disease, the system could provide a detailed explanation, stating that the prediction is based on a combination of factors such as age, medical history, and recent test results.

The push for explainability is not just a technical challenge but also an ethical and legal imperative. Regulations like the European Union's General Data Protection Regulation (GDPR) include provisions for the "right to explanation," allowing individuals to seek more information about decisions made by automated systems that affect them. This regulatory landscape makes XAI even more crucial for organizations that use AI to make decisions impacting individuals' lives or livelihoods.

However, it's essential to note that achieving full transparency and explainability in AI is a complex task that often involves trade-offs. More transparent models may be less accurate or less efficient than their "black box" counterparts. Therefore, the challenge is to find the right balance between performance and explainability, depending on the specific requirements and risks associated with each application.

As AI systems continue to grow in complexity and influence, the need for transparency and explainability becomes increasingly urgent. Explainable AI aims to bridge the gap between human understanding and machine decision-making, making it possible for us to trust and responsibly use these powerful technologies. Whether it's a doctor diagnosing a patient, a project manager overseeing a complex initiative, or a citizen affected by automated legal decisions, XAI offers a path toward more ethical, understandable, and ultimately, acceptable AI.

AI and the Internet of Things (IoT)

The integration of Artificial Intelligence (AI) with the Internet of Things (IoT) is a game-changing development that promises to redefine the boundaries of data collection and analysis in project management. While each of these technologies offers significant benefits on its own, their combined capabilities could revolutionize fields like real-time monitoring and predictive maintenance, making project management more efficient, effective, and agile than ever before.

IoT devices, ranging from simple sensors to complex industrial machinery, can collect vast amounts of data from the physical world. These devices can monitor everything from temperature and humidity in a storage facility to the performance metrics of a manufacturing line. Traditionally, the data collected by these devices would be sent to a centralized system for periodic analysis. However, the integration of AI algorithms directly into IoT devices—or at the edge, in technical parlance—transforms this model by enabling real-time data analysis and decision-making.

For instance, consider a construction project where various IoT sensors are deployed across the site to monitor factors like material integrity, equipment usage, and worker safety. An AI algorithm integrated with these sensors could analyze this data in real-time to identify potential issues before they become critical problems. If a sensor detects that a piece of machinery is overheating, the AI algorithm could immediately alert the project manager and even suggest specific maintenance actions. This real-time monitoring capability could prevent costly equipment breakdowns and enhance worker safety, thereby improving both the efficiency and effectiveness of the project.

Predictive maintenance is another field that stands to benefit immensely from the integration of AI and IoT. In traditional maintenance models, equipment is serviced at regular intervals regardless of its actual condition, leading to unnecessary downtime and resource expenditure. With AI-powered IoT devices, it's possible to move to a predictive maintenance model where equipment is serviced based on its actual condition rather than a predetermined schedule. The AI algorithm can analyze historical and real-time data from IoT sensors to predict when a piece of equipment is likely to fail, allowing for timely intervention. This not only extends the lifespan of the equipment but also minimizes downtime, leading to more efficient project execution.

The potential applications of AI and IoT integration in project management are not limited to construction or manufacturing; they span multiple sectors including healthcare, logistics, and even software development. For example, in a healthcare project aimed at patient monitoring, AI-powered IoT devices could provide real-time analysis of patient data, enabling immediate intervention in critical situations. In logistics, IoT sensors can track the location and condition of shipments in real-time, and AI algorithms can optimize routes and schedules for maximum efficiency.

However, the integration of AI with IoT also presents challenges, particularly in terms of data security and privacy. The increased connectivity and data flow between devices and systems elevate the risk of cyberattacks. Moreover, the real-time decision-making capabilities of AI algorithms could have unintended consequences if not properly managed and monitored. Therefore, robust security protocols and ethical guidelines are essential for the responsible deployment of AI and IoT in project management.

The integration of AI with IoT devices opens up new frontiers in data collection and analysis, offering transformative possibilities for real-time monitoring and predictive maintenance in project management. By enabling more timely and data-driven decision-making, this integration has the potential to make projects more efficient, cost-effective, and agile, revolutionizing project management across a multitude of sectors.

Section 2: Opportunities for Project Managers

Real-time Decision-making

The landscape of project management is undergoing a seismic shift, driven in part by advancements in Artificial Intelligence and computational power. Traditional project management often relies on periodic reviews and updates, where decisions are made based on data that may already be outdated by the time it's analyzed. However, the advent of advanced AI algorithms, coupled with unprecedented computational capabilities, is setting the stage for a more dynamic and responsive approach to project management, one where real-time decision-making becomes not just feasible but standard practice.

Imagine a project management environment where an AI system continuously monitors a wide array of data points, from team performance metrics and resource allocation to stakeholder feedback and market trends. This system doesn't just passively collect data; it actively analyzes it in real-time, using advanced machine learning algorithms to identify patterns, anomalies, and opportunities. For example, if the AI system detects that a particular task is taking longer than expected based on historical data and current conditions, it could immediately flag this issue for review, allowing project managers to intervene before a minor delay turns into a major setback.

The implications of this real-time decision-making capability are profound. Project managers could dynamically adjust resource allocation based on current needs and performance, rather than sticking to a static plan. If the AI system identifies that a particular team member has a lighter workload and the skills necessary for a task that's falling behind schedule, it could suggest reallocating that individual to address the bottleneck. This kind of fluid, responsive resource management could significantly improve project efficiency and outcomes.

Moreover, real-time decision-making extends beyond internal project metrics to encompass external factors as well. Advanced AI algorithms could analyze market trends, customer feedback, and even geopolitical events to assess their potential impact on the project. For instance, if a sudden market shift makes a planned project feature less relevant, the AI system could flag this change immediately, enabling the project team to pivot before investing more time and resources into a less valuable endeavor.

Increased computational power plays a critical role in enabling this real-time analysis. The sheer volume of data that needs to be processed and analyzed for dynamic project management is staggering. Traditional computing systems would struggle to handle this load in a timely manner, but modern, high-performance computing platforms can crunch these numbers in real-time, enabling the kind of rapid, data-driven decision-making that can adapt to changing conditions on the fly.

Of course, the move towards real-time decision-making in project management also presents challenges. It requires a cultural shift within organizations, as team members and stakeholders must become comfortable with a more dynamic, fluid approach to project execution. There may also be technical challenges in integrating advanced AI and computing capabilities with existing project management systems and processes. However, the potential benefits—greater efficiency, more responsive decision-making, and ultimately, more successful projects—make this a compelling direction for the future of project management.

The combination of advanced AI algorithms and increased computational power is opening the door to a new era of project management, one characterized by real-time decision-making based on a wide array of data points. This dynamic approach promises to make project management more responsive and effective, enabling organizations to adapt to changing conditions and seize new opportunities like never before.

Hyper-Personalized Stakeholder Management

The role of a project manager is multifaceted, encompassing not just technical oversight but also intricate human dynamics, particularly in stakeholder engagement. Stakeholders can include anyone from team members and customers to investors and regulatory bodies. Each comes with their own set of expectations, preferences, and concerns, making stakeholder management one of the most complex aspects of project management. As Artificial Intelligence continues to evolve, its potential to revolutionize this area is becoming increasingly clear. Future AI systems could offer unprecedented capabilities in analyzing a wide array of data about stakeholders, thereby enabling project managers to tailor their engagement strategies with a level of precision and effectiveness that was previously unimaginable.

Imagine an AI system that can analyze years of email correspondence, meeting minutes, and even verbal interactions to understand the communication styles of different stakeholders. Some may prefer concise, data-driven communication, while others may value a more narrative, relationship-focused approach. By understanding these preferences, the AI system could automatically generate communication templates or suggest engagement strategies that are most likely to resonate with each stakeholder. This level of personalization could significantly improve the quality of interactions, leading to stronger relationships and more successful project outcomes.

But the potential of AI in stakeholder management goes beyond just communication styles. The system could also analyze past interactions to identify patterns or trends that might inform future engagement. For example, if a particular stakeholder has consistently raised concerns about project timelines, the AI system could flag this as a priority issue for future discussions with that stakeholder. Alternatively, if the AI system detects that a stakeholder's engagement level has dropped—perhaps they are not responding to communications as quickly as they used to or are less active in meetings—it could alert the project manager to take proactive steps to re-engage that individual.

Moreover, AI could integrate data from a variety of sources to provide a more holistic view of stakeholders. For instance, it could analyze social media activity to gauge stakeholder sentiment about a project or industry trends, or it could incorporate market data to provide context for stakeholder concerns or suggestions. By synthesizing this diverse array of data, AI could help project managers not only understand what their stakeholders want but also why they want it, which is crucial for more nuanced and effective engagement.

The ethical implications of such in-depth data analysis are, of course, a critical consideration. Stakeholder data would need to be handled with the utmost care, respecting privacy laws and ethical norms. Transparency would be key; stakeholders should be aware that their data is being analyzed for the purpose of improving project outcomes and should have the option to opt-out if they choose.

As AI systems become more advanced, their potential to transform stakeholder engagement in project management is immense. By analyzing a vast array of data about stakeholders, from communication styles to past interactions and more, AI could enable project managers to tailor their engagement strategies with unprecedented effectiveness. This could lead to stronger relationships, more successful projects, and a more nuanced understanding of the complex human dynamics that are at the heart of any project.

AI in Agile and DevOps

The rise of Agile and DevOps methodologies in software development and IT operations has revolutionized the way organizations approach project management and product delivery. These methodologies prioritize flexibility, collaboration, and rapid iteration, enabling teams to adapt to changing requirements and market conditions more effectively than traditional, waterfall-based approaches. As powerful as Agile and DevOps are on their own, the integration of Artificial Intelligence into these frameworks can supercharge their capabilities, automating routine tasks and providing real-time insights that make these approaches even more efficient.

In an Agile environment, for example, project managers and development teams often have to juggle multiple tasks, from backlog grooming and sprint planning to performance tracking and stakeholder communication. While human expertise is irreplaceable for tasks that require creativity, strategic thinking, and nuanced understanding, many routine tasks can be automated using AI. For instance, AI algorithms can sift through large amounts of project data to automatically prioritize tasks based on predefined criteria such as urgency, dependencies, and team availability. This automation frees up valuable time for project managers and team members, allowing them to focus on more complex and impactful work.

Similarly, in a DevOps context, the continuous integration and continuous delivery (CI/CD) pipeline involves several repetitive tasks such as code testing, deployment, and monitoring. AI can automate many of these tasks, identifying errors more quickly than manual methods and even predicting issues before they occur based on historical data. This not only speeds up the development cycle but also improves the quality of the end product by reducing the likelihood of human error.

Beyond automation, AI can provide real-time insights that are invaluable for Agile and DevOps teams. Machine learning algorithms can analyze historical project data to forecast potential delays, bottlenecks, or resource constraints, allowing teams to take proactive measures before problems escalate. In DevOps, AI-driven analytics tools can monitor system performance in real-time, providing instant feedback that can be used to optimize code, allocate resources more efficiently, or troubleshoot issues before they affect end-users.

The integration of AI into Agile and DevOps is not just a matter of enhancing efficiency; it also has the potential to transform the way teams collaborate and make decisions. With AI providing real-time insights, team members can engage in more informed and focused discussions, leading to better decision-making and, ultimately, more successful project outcomes. Moreover, as AI systems learn from each project, they become increasingly effective at providing recommendations, further enhancing their value over time.

As Agile and DevOps methodologies continue to gain traction across industries, the role of AI in augmenting these approaches is becoming increasingly significant. By automating routine tasks and providing real-time, data-driven insights, AI allows Agile and DevOps teams to operate more efficiently, make better decisions, and focus on the creative and strategic tasks that humans do best. The synergy between AI, Agile, and DevOps represents a promising frontier for project management and software development, offering opportunities for increased efficiency, improved quality, and more successful project outcomes.

Section 3: Challenges and Risks

Ethical and Social Challenges

As Artificial Intelligence systems continue to permeate various aspects of society, from healthcare and education to transportation and commerce, the ethical challenges that accompany this technological revolution are becoming more pronounced and complex. Two issues that stand out in this context are algorithmic bias and job displacement, both of which have far-reaching implications for social equity, economic stability, and the moral fabric of our communities.

Algorithmic bias is a particularly insidious challenge because it can perpetuate and even exacerbate existing social inequalities. When AI systems are trained on data that reflects historical biases, those systems can produce outputs that are similarly biased. For instance, an AI system used in criminal justice that has been trained on past arrest records may disproportionately flag individuals from marginalized communities as potential risks. Similarly, AI algorithms used in hiring may inadvertently discriminate against certain groups if they are trained on data that reflects existing workplace inequalities. The consequences of such biases are not merely academic; they can affect people's lives in profound ways, from limiting their economic opportunities to affecting their interactions with law enforcement.

Job displacement is another ethical challenge that is becoming increasingly pressing as AI systems become more capable and versatile. Automation has always been a driver of economic change, but the advent of highly intelligent systems that can perform tasks that were previously the exclusive domain of humans raises new and urgent questions. While automation can lead to increased efficiency and economic growth, it also has the potential to displace workers on a large scale, particularly those in low-skilled jobs. This displacement can lead to economic inequality, social unrest, and a host of other societal challenges. Moreover, the rapid pace at which AI is advancing makes it difficult for the job market and educational systems to adapt, leaving many people vulnerable to unemployment and underemployment.

Addressing these ethical challenges requires a multi-disciplinary approach that brings together technologists, ethicists, policymakers, and community leaders. It's not enough to develop technical solutions for reducing bias in algorithms; we also need to consider the broader social and economic systems in which these algorithms operate. Similarly, mitigating the impact of job displacement involves more than just retraining programs; it requires a comprehensive economic strategy that addresses the needs of those who are most vulnerable to the negative impacts of automation.

As AI systems become more integrated into the fabric of our society, the ethical challenges we face will become more complex and urgent. Algorithmic bias and job displacement are not just technical issues to be solved by engineers; they are societal challenges that require collective action. By acknowledging the ethical implications of AI and taking proactive steps to address them, we can strive for a future in which technology serves as a force for social good, rather than as a catalyst for inequality and division.

Security Risks

The integration of Artificial Intelligence into project management is a double-edged sword. On one hand, it offers unprecedented capabilities for efficiency, data analysis, and decision-making. On the other hand, the very features that make AI so valuable also make it an attractive target for cyberattacks. As AI systems often have access to sensitive data and critical operational processes, they present a lucrative opportunity for cybercriminals looking to exploit vulnerabilities for financial or strategic gain. This evolving cybersecurity landscape necessitates a heightened sense of vigilance from project managers overseeing AI-driven initiatives.

In the past, project managers might have considered cybersecurity to be primarily the domain of IT specialists. However, as AI becomes more deeply woven into the fabric of project management, the responsibility for cybersecurity is increasingly shared. Project managers now find themselves at the intersection of technology and business, making them key players in the organization's broader cybersecurity strategy. They are often the first line of defense, responsible for identifying potential risks and vulnerabilities within their projects and taking proactive steps to mitigate them.

The complexity of AI systems adds another layer of challenge to maintaining cybersecurity. Unlike traditional software, AI algorithms are not static; they learn and evolve over time. This dynamic nature can introduce new vulnerabilities that were not present during the initial security assessments. Furthermore, AI systems often interact with multiple other systems—both internal and external—increasing the number of potential entry points for cyberattacks. This interconnectedness means that a vulnerability in one system could potentially compromise the integrity of the entire project or even the broader organization.

Given these challenges, project managers will need to adopt a multi-faceted approach to cybersecurity. This involves not just technical solutions like firewalls, encryption, and regular software updates, but also organizational strategies such as employee training, regular security audits, and the establishment of clear protocols for reporting and responding to security incidents. Project managers will need to work closely with cybersecurity experts to ensure that all team members are aware of the latest threats and best practices for safeguarding against them. They will also need to foster a culture of cybersecurity within their teams, where vigilance and awareness are ingrained values.

Moreover, as cyber threats continue to evolve, project managers will need to stay updated on the latest cybersecurity trends and technologies. This may require ongoing training and perhaps even specialized certifications in cybersecurity as it relates to AI. It's not just about preventing unauthorized access to systems; it's also about ensuring the ethical handling of data, protecting intellectual property, and maintaining the trust of stakeholders and customers.

The increasing integration of AI into project management is changing the cybersecurity landscape in profound ways. Project managers can no longer afford to be passive observers, relying solely on IT departments to protect their projects. They must take an active role in identifying vulnerabilities, implementing safeguards, and maintaining a state of constant vigilance against the ever-present threat of cyberattacks. As AI continues to transform the field of project management, a robust approach to cybersecurity will be not just beneficial but essential for the success and integrity of projects.

Skill Gap and Training

As Artificial Intelligence continues its rapid evolution, the role of project managers in overseeing AI-driven initiatives is becoming increasingly complex and nuanced. Gone are the days when a rudimentary understanding of AI concepts was sufficient. Today's project managers are finding that they need to delve deeper into the intricacies of AI technologies to effectively manage projects from inception to completion. This shift is not merely a trend but a necessity, driven by the growing sophistication of AI tools and the multifaceted challenges they bring to the table.

In the early days of AI adoption, project managers could often rely on specialized AI teams to handle the technical details, while they focused on broader project objectives, timelines, and resource allocation. However, as AI technologies become more integrated into various aspects of business operations, project managers can no longer afford to be passive intermediaries between technical and non-technical stakeholders. They must acquire a more comprehensive understanding of how AI algorithms work, how data should be managed, and how AI outputs should be interpreted. This deeper understanding enables them to ask the right questions, identify potential pitfalls, and make more informed decisions.

The need for ongoing education and training in advanced AI concepts is becoming increasingly apparent. This is not just about understanding the latest machine learning algorithms or data analytics tools, but also about grasping the ethical, legal, and social implications of AI. For instance, as AI systems are increasingly used in decision-making processes, project managers need to understand the risks of algorithmic bias, the importance of data privacy, and the ethical considerations of automated decision-making. This multifaceted understanding of AI allows project managers to serve as effective bridges between technical experts, ethical advisors, legal teams, and business leaders, ensuring that projects are not only technically sound but also ethically and legally compliant.

Ongoing education and training can take various forms, from formal academic courses and certifications to workshops, webinars, and on-the-job training. Importantly, this education should not be viewed as a one-time activity but as a continuous process. The field of AI is dynamic, with new advancements and challenges emerging regularly. Project managers need to adopt a mindset of lifelong learning, continually updating their knowledge and skills to stay relevant.

Moreover, as AI tools become more user-friendly and accessible, project managers may find themselves directly interacting with these tools, tweaking algorithms, or even running simulations. In such scenarios, a lack of advanced understanding could lead to suboptimal decisions and outcomes. Therefore, the onus is on both individual project managers and the organizations they work for to invest in ongoing education and training programs that equip them with the skills needed to navigate the evolving landscape of AI effectively.

The growing sophistication of AI tools is ushering in a new era of project management—one that requires a deeper, more nuanced understanding of advanced AI concepts. This necessitates a commitment to ongoing education and training, enabling project managers to lead AI projects with the expertise and confidence required in this dynamic and complex field.

Section 4: Case Studies

Case Study 1: Quantum Computing in Aerospace Project Management

Introduction

The aerospace industry is known for its complex engineering challenges that require high levels of computational power. Traditional computing methods, while effective, often require extensive time and resources, especially for intricate simulations like airflow over an aircraft wing or rocket trajectory calculations. This case study explores how an aerospace company is leveraging quantum computing to optimize these complex simulations, resulting in drastic reductions in project timelines.

Background

The aerospace company in focus is a leading player in the industry, involved in both commercial and defense projects. With the increasing demand for more efficient and safer aircraft, the company has been investing in advanced technologies to stay competitive. One such investment is in quantum computing, a technology that promises unprecedented computational capabilities. The company initiated a project aimed at integrating quantum computing into its simulation processes, which traditionally took weeks or even months to complete using classical computing methods.

Challenges and Objectives
Challenges
- Computational Complexity: Aerospace simulations involve solving highly complex equations that are computationally intensive.
- Time Constraints: Traditional computing methods could take an extended period, delaying the overall project timeline.
- Resource Allocation: The computational demands often required dedicated supercomputing resources, which are expensive to maintain.

Objectives
- Speed: To drastically reduce the time required for complex simulations.
- Accuracy: To maintain or improve the accuracy of the simulations.
- Cost-Efficiency: To optimize resource allocation, thereby reducing costs.

Approach and Implementation
Preliminary Research and Team Formation
The company started by forming a specialized team of aerospace engineers, quantum computing experts, and project managers. Initial research was conducted to identify the types of simulations that would benefit most from quantum computing.

Partnering with Quantum Computing Providers
Recognizing the need for specialized hardware, the company partnered with a leading quantum computing provider. This collaboration allowed them to access cutting-edge quantum processors and expertise.

Algorithm Development
The team developed new algorithms tailored for quantum computing. These algorithms were designed to solve the complex equations involved in aerospace simulations more efficiently than classical methods.

Testing and Validation
Before full-scale implementation, the algorithms underwent rigorous testing. Initial tests were conducted on smaller problems to validate the algorithm's efficacy, followed by more extensive tests on larger, more complex simulations.

Integration and Scaling
Once validated, the quantum algorithms were integrated into the company's existing simulation software. The project then moved into the scaling phase, where it was rolled out to different departments and project teams.

Outcomes and Impact
Time Savings: The use of quantum computing reduced the simulation time from weeks to days, and in some cases, even hours.

- Increased Accuracy: The new algorithms provided more accurate results, enhancing the reliability of the simulations.
- Cost-Efficiency: The reduced time for simulations allowed for better resource allocation, leading to cost savings.
- Competitive Advantage: The successful implementation of quantum computing has given the company a significant edge over competitors still relying on classical computing methods.

Lessons Learned and Future Directions
The project was not without its challenges, including the steep learning curve associated with quantum computing and initial resistance from engineers accustomed to classical methods. However, the benefits have clearly outweighed the challenges, validating the company's investment in quantum computing.

The company plans to continue its research in quantum computing, exploring other applications beyond simulations. There is also a plan to collaborate with academic institutions to advance the field further.

Conclusion
This case study demonstrates the transformative potential of quantum computing in the aerospace industry. By successfully integrating quantum algorithms into their simulation processes, the company has not only drastically reduced project timelines but also gained a competitive advantage in an industry where speed and accuracy are paramount. The experience offers valuable insights for other industries facing similar computational challenges and looking to explore the benefits of quantum computing.

Case Study 2: AI Ethics in Smart City Development

Introduction
Smart cities are at the forefront of using technology to improve the quality of life for their citizens. However, the use of Artificial Intelligence (AI) in these projects brings forth complex ethical considerations. This case study examines how a smart city project is implementing ethical AI algorithms to ensure equitable resource allocation among its diverse population. The focus is on how

the city's project managers, in collaboration with AI experts, ethicists, and community stakeholders, are navigating the ethical landscape to create a more inclusive and fair urban environment.

Background

The smart city in question aims to be a global model for integrating technology into urban planning and governance. One of its flagship initiatives is to use AI algorithms for resource allocation in areas such as public transportation, healthcare, and education. While the promise of efficiency and optimization is high, so is the potential for perpetuating existing inequalities if not carefully managed. The city's diverse population, with varying needs and access to resources, makes the ethical implementation of AI a top priority.

Ethical Considerations and Challenges

The project identified several ethical considerations that needed to be addressed:

- Data Privacy: The AI algorithms would require access to a large amount of citizen data, raising concerns about data privacy and security.
- Algorithmic Fairness: The diverse demographic makeup of the city meant that the algorithms had to be designed to prevent any form of discrimination or bias.
- Transparency and Accountability: The decision-making process of the algorithms needed to be transparent, and mechanisms for accountability had to be in place.
- Community Involvement: Given that the algorithms would have a direct impact on citizens' lives, their involvement in the decision-making process was considered crucial.

Approach and Implementation
Collaborative Framework

The project adopted a collaborative approach, bringing together a cross-disciplinary team of project managers, AI experts, ethicists, and community representatives. This ensured a holistic perspective on both the technical and ethical aspects of the project.

Ethical Guidelines and Principles

The team developed a set of ethical guidelines and principles that would govern the design and implementation of the AI algorithms. These were rooted in the broader ethical framework of fairness, transparency, and community involvement.

Data Collection and Algorithm Design

Special attention was given to the data collection process to ensure representativeness and prevent bias. The algorithm was designed to be fairness-aware, with periodic audits to assess its impact on different demographic groups.

Transparency Measures

To ensure transparency, the project included a public dashboard that displayed real-time data on resource allocation. This was complemented by an annual report detailing the algorithm's decision-making process and impact.

Community Feedback Loop

A community feedback mechanism was implemented, allowing citizens to report any issues or biases they experienced. This feedback was used to make ongoing adjustments to the algorithm.

Outcomes and Impact

Since its implementation, the project has seen several positive outcomes:

- Increased Public Trust: The transparent and ethical approach has led to increased trust among citizens.
- Equitable Resource Allocation: Preliminary data indicates a more equitable distribution of resources across different demographic groups.
- Regulatory Compliance: The ethical framework has helped the project comply with existing and emerging regulations on data privacy and algorithmic fairness.
- Global Recognition: The project has received international acclaim as a model for ethical AI implementation in smart cities.

Lessons Learned and Future Directions

The project faced several challenges, including data quality issues and initial resistance from some stakeholders. However, the collaborative and ethical approach has proven to be effective in navigating these challenges.

Going forward, the project plans to continuously update its ethical guidelines in response to technological advancements and societal changes. It also aims to expand the community feedback mechanism to include more diverse voices.

Conclusion

The case study demonstrates that ethical considerations are not just an add-on but an integral part of AI implementation in smart city projects. By adopting a collaborative and principle-based approach, the project has been able to ensure not just the efficiency but also the equity of its resource allocation algorithms. This offers valuable insights for other smart cities aiming to implement AI in an ethical and inclusive manner.

Section 5: Preparing for the Future: Recommendations for Project Managers

Continuous Learning

The velocity at which the field of Artificial Intelligence is advancing is nothing short of breathtaking. New algorithms are being developed, existing ones are being refined, and novel applications are emerging across industries at an unprecedented rate. For project managers who are tasked with overseeing AI projects, this rapid evolution presents both an opportunity and a challenge. The opportunity lies in harnessing the transformative power of AI to drive innovation and efficiency. The challenge, however, is in keeping pace with the ever-changing landscape of AI technologies, methodologies, and ethical considerations.

In this dynamic environment, the concept of 'continuous learning' takes on a new level of urgency for project managers. Unlike more static fields where one can rely on established best practices and stable technologies, AI is a domain of constant flux. What was considered state-of-the-art six months ago may already be outdated, and ethical guidelines and legal regulations are continually evolving to catch up with technological advancements.

Continuous learning for project managers in the context of AI is not just about understanding the technical aspects, although that is certainly important. It's also about understanding the broader ecosystem in which AI operates. This includes staying abreast of emerging ethical considerations, understanding the societal and cultural implications of AI, and keeping up-to-date with relevant laws and regulations. For instance, as discussions around algorithmic bias or data privacy gain traction, project managers need to be well-versed in these topics to ensure that their projects are not just technically sound but also ethically responsible and legally compliant.

This commitment to continuous learning may involve a variety of activities and strategies. Formal education, such as specialized training courses in AI ethics or data science, can provide a strong foundational understanding. Webinars, workshops, and conferences can offer more timely insights into the latest developments in the field. Online forums, social media platforms, and academic journals can be valuable resources for staying up-to-date with the most recent research and discussions. Networking with AI experts, ethicists, and other professionals can also provide nuanced perspectives that are crucial for informed decision-making.

Moreover, continuous learning is not just an individual endeavor but should be integrated into the organizational culture. Project managers can take the lead in fostering an environment that values ongoing education, perhaps by organizing regular knowledge-sharing sessions or by advocating for company-wide training programs in AI ethics and technologies.

In a field as dynamic and impactful as AI, the concept of 'learning on the job' takes on a whole new meaning. It's not just about solving the challenges that arise during the course of a project, but also about anticipating the challenges that are yet to come. For project managers, this means a commitment to continuous learning is not just beneficial but essential for successfully navigating the complex and rapidly evolving landscape of AI.

Ethical Leadership

The ethical implementation of Artificial Intelligence in projects is becoming a focal point of concern and scrutiny, and rightly so. As the individuals responsible for overseeing the entire lifecycle of a project, project managers are increasingly finding themselves at the intersection of technology and ethics. They are the ones who must ensure that AI is not just implemented efficiently and effectively, but also ethically. This is a multifaceted responsibility that extends from the initial stages of data collection all the way to the point where algorithms make critical decisions.

In the realm of data collection, project managers must ensure that the data used to train and validate AI models is gathered and handled in an ethical manner. This involves not just compliance with data protection laws, but also a consideration of the fairness and representativeness of the data. For example, if an AI system is being developed to screen job applicants, the project manager must ensure that the data used to train the system does not reflect historical biases against certain demographic groups. This may involve working closely with data scientists to review the data sources, as well as consulting with ethicists or diversity and inclusion experts to assess the potential for bias.

Once data collection is complete, the ethical considerations continue into the development and training of the AI algorithms. Here, project managers must work with AI experts to ensure that the algorithms do not perpetuate or amplify existing biases in the data. This could involve the use of fairness-aware machine learning techniques, or the implementation of regular audits to assess the algorithm's decisions for potential bias. Project managers may also need to liaise with legal teams to ensure that the algorithm complies with regulations related to algorithmic decision-making and discrimination.

But ethical considerations don't end once the AI system is developed; they extend into the deployment and operational phases as well. When AI systems are put into practice, project managers must ensure that there are mechanisms in place for transparency and accountability. If an AI system is used to make decisions that affect people's lives, such as medical diagnoses or loan approvals, it's crucial that those decisions can be explained and justified. This is particularly challenging given the 'black box' nature of many AI algorithms, which make decisions based on complex computations that are not easily interpretable by humans. Project managers may need to work with AI experts to implement explainability features or to develop user interfaces that clearly communicate how decisions are made.

Furthermore, project managers must also consider the long-term ethical implications of AI systems. This could involve setting up ongoing monitoring to assess the real-world impact of the AI system, or establishing a feedback loop where end-users can report issues or concerns related to ethical considerations such as fairness, transparency, or privacy.

In essence, the role of the project manager in the ethical implementation of AI is expansive and continuous. It requires a proactive approach to ethics, starting from the earliest stages of a project and continuing through its entire lifecycle. This involves collaboration with a wide range of stakeholders, from data scientists and AI experts to ethicists, legal advisors, and end-users. It's a challenging but critically important role that will increasingly define the success and societal impact of AI projects.

Collaboration with AI Experts

As Artificial Intelligence systems continue to evolve in complexity and capability, the role of project managers is undergoing a significant transformation. Gone are the days when project managers could operate with only a cursory understanding of the technologies they were overseeing. The intricacies of modern AI systems demand a deeper level of technical insight, not necessarily to the point of becoming an AI expert, but certainly enough to understand the nuances, limitations, and ethical implications of the technology. This is particularly true for project managers who are responsible for implementing and managing AI-driven projects, where the stakes are often high and the margin for error is slim.

The increasing complexity of AI systems manifests in various ways. For instance, machine learning models are becoming more sophisticated, capable of analyzing vast and diverse data sets to make predictions or decisions that could have far-reaching consequences. Natural language processing algorithms are advancing to the point where they can understand and generate human-like text, raising questions about authenticity and the potential for misuse. Computer vision technologies are being deployed in everything from autonomous vehicles to healthcare diagnostics, requiring rigorous testing and validation to ensure they meet safety and accuracy standards.

Given these complexities, project managers can no longer afford to work in a silo. Collaboration with AI experts becomes not just beneficial but essential for the successful implementation and management of AI projects. AI experts can provide the technical guidance needed to navigate the complexities of the technology, from data collection and model training to validation and deployment. They can also offer valuable insights into the ethical considerations that come with AI use, such as data privacy, algorithmic bias, and transparency.

But this collaboration is not a one-way street. Just as project managers need the technical insights of AI experts, so too do AI experts need the organizational and managerial skills that project managers bring to the table. Implementing an AI system is not just a technical exercise; it's a complex project that requires careful planning, coordination among various stakeholders, and rigorous risk management. Project managers can help ensure that the project stays on track, on time, and on budget, while also navigating the organizational and ethical complexities that often arise.

Moreover, as AI technologies become more integrated into the core operations of an organization, the role of the project manager may expand to include ongoing oversight and management of AI systems. This could involve regular collaboration with AI experts to update and refine the algorithms, ensure compliance with evolving regulations, and assess the long-term impact and effectiveness of the technology.

As AI systems grow in complexity, the role of the project manager is evolving to require a deeper level of technical and ethical understanding. This, in turn, necessitates closer collaboration with AI experts, creating a symbiotic relationship where each brings their unique skills and insights to the table. Together, they can more effectively navigate the complexities of implementing and managing AI systems, ensuring not only the technical success of the project but also its ethical and organizational integrity.

Conclusion: The Future is Now

The future of AI in project management is not a distant reality; it's unfolding now. By staying informed about emerging trends, seizing new opportunities, and navigating challenges responsibly, project managers can not only adapt to this changing landscape but also play a pivotal role in shaping it.

CHAPTER 8: IMPLEMENTING AI IN YOUR PROJECT MANAGEMENT PRACTICE: A STEP-BY-STEP GUIDE

Introduction: The Journey to AI Integration

The potential of AI in transforming project management is immense, but the path to successful implementation is often fraught with challenges. From selecting the right tools to training your team and ensuring ethical compliance, there are numerous factors to consider. This chapter serves as a comprehensive, step-by-step guide for project managers looking to integrate AI into their practices.

Section 1: Assessing Your Needs and Readiness

Identifying Pain Points

Before embarking on the journey of integrating Artificial Intelligence (AI) into any project or organizational workflow, it's imperative to have a clear understanding of the specific challenges or inefficiencies you aim to address. Implementing AI without a targeted focus can lead to wasted resources, misaligned objectives, and ultimately, failure to realize the technology's potential benefits. Whether the challenge lies in data analysis, scheduling, stakeholder engagement, or another area, identifying it clearly is the first crucial step in a successful AI implementation strategy.

In the realm of data analysis, for example, the sheer volume of data generated in today's digital age can be overwhelming. Traditional methods of data analysis may not be sufficient to sift through this avalanche of information to derive actionable insights. If your organization faces bottlenecks in processing and interpreting data, AI can be a game-changer. Machine learning algorithms can automate the analysis of large datasets, identifying patterns and trends that might be invisible to the human eye. This could be particularly useful in sectors like healthcare, where rapid and accurate analysis of patient data can directly impact outcomes, or in retail, where understanding consumer behavior patterns can give a competitive edge.

Scheduling is another area where AI can bring transformative benefits. In complex projects with multiple interdependent tasks, resources, and deadlines, even experienced project managers can struggle to optimize scheduling. Traditional methods often rely on fixed algorithms and manual input, making them rigid and time-consuming. AI algorithms can analyze a multitude of variables, such as team availability, task complexity, and historical data, to automatically generate optimized schedules. This not only enhances efficiency but also allows for real-time adjustments to adapt to unforeseen challenges or changes in project scope.

Stakeholder engagement is yet another domain ripe for AI intervention. Managing and communicating with various stakeholders, from team members and clients to vendors and regulatory bodies, is a complex and often delicate task. Poor stakeholder engagement can lead to misunderstandings, delays, and even project failure. AI tools equipped with Natural Language Processing (NLP) can analyze stakeholder communications to gauge sentiment and attitudes, providing a data-driven approach to stakeholder management. They can also automate routine communications, freeing up project managers to focus on more strategic engagement activities.

Beyond these examples, the challenges that AI can address are as diverse as the projects and organizations that may employ it. It could be used for risk assessment in financial portfolios, predictive maintenance in manufacturing, personalized learning paths in education, or countless other applications. The key is to identify the specific challenge or inefficiency that is most pressing for your project or organization.

Once the challenge is identified, the next steps include selecting the appropriate AI technologies and methodologies, gathering and preparing the data, and finally, implementing and iterating the AI solution. Each of these steps comes with its own set of complexities and considerations, from ethical concerns around data usage to the technical challenges of integrating AI into existing systems. However, none of these subsequent steps can be effectively undertaken without first having a crystal-clear understanding of the problem you're aiming to solve.

The first and perhaps most crucial step in any AI implementation strategy is to identify the specific challenges or inefficiencies you aim to address. This focused approach ensures that the AI technologies employed will be aligned with the project or organizational objectives, setting the stage for a successful and impactful implementation.

Evaluating Organizational Readiness

The integration of Artificial Intelligence (AI) into an organization's workflow is not merely a technological endeavor but a holistic transformation that impacts various facets of the organization. Before diving into AI implementation, it's crucial to assess the readiness of your organization on multiple fronts: technical infrastructure, skill levels, and cultural readiness. Each of these elements plays a vital role in determining the success of AI adoption, and a thorough assessment can help you identify gaps and plan for the necessary changes.

Starting with the technical infrastructure, the first question to ask is whether your existing systems are capable of supporting AI technologies. AI algorithms, particularly machine learning models, often require significant computational power and storage capabilities. The data pipelines must be robust enough to handle large volumes of data securely and efficiently. If your current infrastructure is not up to the task, you may need to invest in hardware upgrades or consider cloud-based solutions that can scale with your needs. Additionally, the compatibility of AI solutions with existing software systems must be evaluated to ensure seamless integration. For instance, if you're planning to use AI for data analytics, how well does the chosen AI tool integrate with your existing data storage solutions? Are there APIs or middleware that can facilitate this integration?

Next, assessing skill levels within the organization is paramount. AI technologies often require specialized skills that your current team may not possess. Do you have data scientists who can develop and train machine learning models? Are your engineers familiar with the programming languages and frameworks commonly used in AI development, such as Python, TensorFlow, or PyTorch? If the answer is no, you may need to consider options like hiring new talent, upskilling current employees through training programs, or partnering with external AI experts. Even for non-technical staff, a basic understanding of AI concepts can be beneficial for more effective collaboration and decision-making.

Lastly, but no less important, is the assessment of cultural readiness. The adoption of AI often necessitates a cultural shift within the organization. Employees may have concerns about job displacement due to automation, or there may be resistance to change in general. The leadership team must be committed to guiding this cultural transition, addressing concerns, and fostering an environment that is open to innovation. This could involve internal communications campaigns to educate employees on the benefits of AI, both for the organization and their individual roles. It might also include creating cross-functional teams to oversee AI implementation, ensuring that it aligns with broader organizational goals and values.

Moreover, ethical considerations around AI, such as data privacy and algorithmic bias, should be part of the cultural conversation. Establishing ethical guidelines for AI usage can help in building trust and ensuring responsible adoption. This is not just a task for the technical team but should involve stakeholders from various departments, including legal, HR, and ethics committees if they exist.

Assessing the readiness of your organization for AI adoption is a multi-faceted exercise that goes beyond the mere evaluation of technical capabilities. It requires a deep dive into the skill sets available within your team and an honest look at the cultural dynamics that could either facilitate or hinder successful implementation. By taking the time to thoroughly assess these elements, you can develop a more targeted and effective AI adoption strategy, increasing the likelihood of a successful and impactful transformation.

Tools and Surveys

The adoption of Artificial Intelligence (AI) in an organization is a significant undertaking that requires careful planning and assessment. While internal evaluations are crucial, AI Readiness Assessment Tools can offer a structured, data-driven approach to gauge an organization's preparedness for AI integration. These tools come in various forms, including software platforms, questionnaires, and frameworks, each designed to evaluate different aspects of readiness, from technical infrastructure and skill levels to cultural adaptability.

Software-based AI Readiness Assessment Tools often provide a comprehensive evaluation by scanning your existing IT environment, analyzing hardware capabilities, software compatibility, and data architectures. These tools can generate detailed reports that highlight the strengths and weaknesses of your current infrastructure, offering recommendations for upgrades or modifications. For example, they might suggest the need for more robust data storage solutions or point out bottlenecks in data pipelines that could hinder the performance of AI algorithms. Some of these software tools even offer simulations to predict how your existing systems would handle specific AI workloads, providing valuable insights into necessary upgrades.

Questionnaire-based assessment tools typically focus on the human and organizational aspects of AI readiness. These questionnaires may be distributed to various stakeholders, including executives, project managers, engineers, and even end-users, to gather perspectives on AI adoption. Questions could range from the technical—"Do you have experience with machine learning frameworks?"—to the cultural—"How open is your department to adopting new technologies?" The collected data can then be analyzed to identify gaps in skills or areas where resistance to change might be expected. This qualitative approach complements the quantitative data gathered by software tools, offering a more holistic view of the organization's readiness.

Frameworks for AI readiness often combine elements of both software and questionnaire approaches, providing a structured methodology for assessment. These frameworks may offer step-by-step guides that walk you through various evaluation stages, from initial data gathering to in-depth analysis and final reporting. They often include best practices, case studies, and actionable recommendations tailored to different industries or types of projects. Some frameworks also incorporate financial models to help you estimate the costs associated with AI adoption, from hardware and software investments to training and hiring.

The value of using AI Readiness Assessment Tools lies not just in the data they gather but also in the conversations they spark within the organization. The assessment process itself can serve as a catalyst for internal discussions about strategic goals, potential challenges, and the roadmap for AI adoption. It encourages cross-departmental collaboration and helps align the organization's AI efforts with its broader business objectives.

AI Readiness Assessment Tools offer a structured, comprehensive way to evaluate your organization's preparedness for AI adoption. By combining technical evaluations with human and organizational insights, these tools provide a multi-faceted view of readiness that can inform your AI strategy. Whether you're at the beginning stages of considering AI or already have some initiatives underway, leveraging these assessment tools can provide valuable insights that help you navigate the complex landscape of AI integration.

Skill Gap Analysis: Tools to evaluate the current skill levels against the requirements for AI implementation.

Section 2: Selecting the Right AI Tools

Criteria for Selection

Functionality: Does the tool meet your specific needs?

Usability: Is it user-friendly?

Scalability: Can it grow with your project or organization?

Compliance: Does it meet legal and ethical standards?

Vendor Evaluation

How to assess the credibility, track record, and reliability of AI tool vendors.

Case Studies for Tool Selection

AI in Marketing Projects: How a marketing firm chose an AI tool for customer sentiment analysis.

Introduction
The adoption of Artificial Intelligence (AI) in various industries is no longer a trend but a necessity for staying competitive. In the realm of marketing, AI has been a game-changer, offering unprecedented

insights into customer behavior and sentiment. This case study explores how a mid-sized marketing firm successfully chose and implemented an AI tool for customer sentiment analysis, transforming their approach to client campaigns and achieving remarkable results.

Background

The marketing firm, named MarketMaven, specializes in digital marketing solutions for small and medium-sized enterprises. With a growing client base and an increasing volume of online customer interactions to analyze, the firm found it challenging to keep up using traditional data analysis methods. MarketMaven recognized the need for a more efficient, automated solution to analyze customer sentiment across various digital platforms, from social media to online reviews.

Identifying the Need

MarketMaven's primary challenge was sifting through thousands of customer interactions to gauge public sentiment about their clients' products or services. The manual process was not only time-consuming but also prone to human error and bias. The firm realized that an automated, AI-driven approach could offer more accurate, timely, and actionable insights. The goal was to find an AI tool that could analyze text data from multiple sources and provide a nuanced understanding of customer sentiment, thereby enabling more targeted and effective marketing strategies.

Selection Criteria

The firm established a set of criteria for selecting the AI tool:

- Ease of Integration: The tool needed to integrate seamlessly with existing data storage and analytics platforms.
- Scalability: As the firm was growing, the tool needed to scale without a significant increase in costs.
- Accuracy: The tool's algorithms had to offer high accuracy in sentiment analysis.
- Compliance and Security: Given the sensitive nature of client data, the tool had to comply with data privacy regulations.
- Cost-Effectiveness: Budget constraints meant the tool had to offer good value for the price.

Market Research and Trials

MarketMaven conducted extensive market research to identify potential AI tools that met their criteria. They shortlisted three tools and initiated a trial period for each. During the trials, they tested the tools on past campaigns to assess their accuracy and ease of use. They also evaluated customer support, documentation, and the frequency of software updates.

Decision and Implementation

After a month-long trial period, MarketMaven chose 'SentimentIQ,' an AI tool specializing in sentiment analysis. SentimentIQ scored highly on accuracy and offered a user-friendly interface. It also provided robust data security features and demonstrated excellent customer support. The firm negotiated a scalable pricing model, making it a cost-effective choice.

The implementation phase involved integrating SentimentIQ with MarketMaven's existing data analytics platforms. A cross-functional team, including data scientists, IT specialists, and marketing experts, oversaw the integration and initial testing.

Outcomes and Impact

Within the first quarter of using SentimentIQ, MarketMaven reported a 25% reduction in the time spent on data analysis, allowing the team to focus more on strategic decision-making. The tool's insights also led to more targeted campaigns, resulting in a 15% increase in customer engagement rates for their clients. Importantly, the AI tool's nuanced sentiment analysis helped identify not just positive and negative sentiments but also customer pain points that had previously gone unnoticed.

Lessons Learned and Future Directions
The experience taught MarketMaven the importance of thorough market research and trial periods when selecting an AI tool. It also highlighted the need for cross-departmental collaboration for successful implementation. Encouraged by the positive outcomes, the firm plans to explore additional AI-driven solutions for other areas of marketing, such as predictive analytics for customer behavior.

Conclusion
The case study demonstrates how a thoughtful approach to selecting an AI tool can yield significant benefits. By identifying their specific needs, setting clear criteria, and conducting rigorous trials, MarketMaven successfully adopted an AI solution that transformed their customer sentiment analysis, leading to more effective and efficient marketing campaigns.

AI in Construction: How a construction company selected a machine learning tool for resource allocation.

Introduction
The construction industry has long been a sector reliant on manual processes and human expertise. However, the advent of Artificial Intelligence (AI) and machine learning technologies is revolutionizing how construction companies manage their projects. This case study delves into the journey of BuildRight, a leading construction company, as it navigated the selection and implementation of a machine learning tool for optimizing resource allocation.

Background
BuildRight is a well-established construction company with a diverse portfolio, ranging from residential buildings to large-scale infrastructure projects. Despite its success, the company faced persistent challenges in resource allocation, including labor, machinery, and materials. Inaccurate or inefficient allocation often led to project delays and cost overruns. Recognizing the need for a more data-driven approach, BuildRight decided to explore machine learning solutions capable of automating and optimizing resource allocation.

Identifying the Need
The primary pain point for BuildRight was the complexity involved in allocating resources across multiple ongoing projects. Traditional methods, often reliant on spreadsheets and human judgment, were becoming increasingly untenable. The company sought a machine learning tool that could analyze various factors—such as project timelines, labor skills, equipment availability, and material lead times—to recommend optimal resource allocation.

Selection Criteria
BuildRight established several criteria for selecting the machine learning tool:

- Accuracy: The tool had to provide reliable and accurate recommendations based on complex data sets.

- User-Friendly Interface: Ease of use was essential to ensure quick adoption by project managers and other stakeholders.
- Scalability: The tool needed to be scalable to accommodate the company's growth and the complexity of larger projects.
- Integration: Seamless integration with existing project management software was a must.
- Compliance and Security: The tool had to meet industry standards for data security and compliance with regulations.

Market Research and Pilot Testing

After conducting market research, BuildRight shortlisted three machine learning tools that met their criteria. The company decided to run pilot tests for each tool on smaller projects. The pilots aimed to assess the tool's effectiveness in real-world conditions, focusing on accuracy, ease of use, and the impact on project efficiency.

Decision and Implementation

Following the pilot tests, BuildRight selected 'OptiBuild,' a machine learning tool designed specifically for the construction industry. OptiBuild excelled in accuracy and offered a user-friendly dashboard that was quickly adopted by the team. The tool also provided robust data encryption and compliance features, ensuring data security.

The implementation phase involved training sessions for project managers and integration with BuildRight's existing project management software. A dedicated team was formed to oversee the implementation and address any teething issues.

Outcomes and Impact

Within six months of implementing OptiBuild, BuildRight observed a 20% improvement in project efficiency and a 15% reduction in costs related to resource wastage. The tool's real-time analytics also enabled proactive adjustments, significantly reducing project delays. Additionally, the machine learning algorithms continually improved their recommendations as more data was fed into the system, leading to increasingly optimized resource allocation over time.

Lessons Learned and Future Directions

The successful implementation of OptiBuild taught BuildRight several valuable lessons. Firstly, the importance of pilot testing to validate the tool's capabilities in real-world conditions. Secondly, the need for cross-functional collaboration to ensure successful implementation and adoption across the organization.

Encouraged by the success of OptiBuild, BuildRight is now exploring other AI applications, such as predictive maintenance and safety analytics, to further enhance project efficiency and outcomes.

Conclusion

This case study illustrates the transformative potential of machine learning in the construction industry. By carefully selecting a tool that met its specific needs and criteria, BuildRight was able to significantly improve its resource allocation, leading to more efficient and cost-effective projects. The experience serves as a blueprint for other construction companies looking to leverage AI for operational excellence.

Section 3: Training and Skill Development

Training Programs

The integration of Artificial Intelligence (AI) tools into an organization's workflow is a complex process that extends beyond the realm of technical implementation. It's a human-centric endeavor that necessitates a comprehensive training strategy. Ensuring that your team is proficient in using these sophisticated tools is vital for the successful adoption and effective utilization of AI technologies. A well-rounded training program can be a combination of online and in-person educational experiences, each offering unique benefits that contribute to a smooth transition and effective tool usage.

Online training programs are convenient because they allow team members to learn at their own pace and according to their own schedules. These programs often take the form of interactive courses, webinars, or video tutorials and are particularly useful for remote teams or organizations spread across multiple locations. Specialized courses on online platforms focus on specific AI tools or applications, offering a blend of theoretical and practical knowledge. Live webinars provide an opportunity for real-time interaction with experts, including live demonstrations and Q&A sessions. Many online courses also offer certification upon completion, which can serve as a recognized credential to boost team morale and individual career paths.

In contrast, in-person training sessions offer a more hands-on and interactive learning experience. These are particularly effective for complex AI tools that require a deep level of technical understanding. Workshops led by experts offer an in-depth look into specific features or applications of the AI tool, often including real-world examples and live demonstrations. Intensive training bootcamps provide a comprehensive understanding of the tool in a condensed timeframe, making it a fast-track option for teams that need to get up to speed quickly. Some companies even offer the option of onsite training, where experts come to your location to provide highly customized training tailored to your organization's specific needs.

A blended approach that combines the benefits of both online and in-person training can offer a flexible, tailored training program that caters to varying skill levels and learning paces within your team. Team members can start with online courses to learn the basics and then transition to in-person sessions for more advanced, hands-on training.

It's important to note that AI is a rapidly evolving field, and AI tools are often updated with new features and capabilities. Therefore, ongoing training is essential for staying current. Many organizations opt for a subscription-based training model, which provides access to updated courses and materials as the AI tools themselves evolve.

A well-structured training program is crucial for the successful implementation and adoption of new AI tools. By leveraging a mix of online and in-person training methods, you can ensure that your team is well-equipped to maximize the benefits of these advanced technologies, leading to more efficient and effective project outcomes.

Skill Development Strategies

Internal Workshops: Conduct workshops led by AI experts.

Online Courses: Utilize online platforms that offer courses on AI and machine learning.

Certification Programs: Encourage team members to earn AI-related certifications.

Section 4: Implementation and Integration

Pilot Testing

efore diving into a full-scale implementation of an Artificial Intelligence (AI) tool, it's imperative to conduct a pilot test. This preliminary phase serves multiple purposes, including evaluating the tool's effectiveness and identifying any issues that may arise during broader deployment. A pilot test acts as a safety net, allowing you to make informed decisions based on real-world data and user experiences, rather than relying solely on vendor promises or theoretical capabilities.

The first step in conducting a pilot test is to select a smaller, manageable project or a specific segment of a larger project as your testing ground. This should be a project that is representative of the kinds of challenges and tasks your team typically faces, but not so critical that any hiccups could be disastrous. The idea is to create a controlled environment where you can closely monitor the AI tool's performance and its impact on project outcomes.

Next, involve key stakeholders in the pilot phase. This includes not just the project managers and team members who will be using the tool, but also any executives or clients who have a vested interest in the project's success. Their feedback can provide valuable insights into how the tool affects not just the workflow but also the end results and client satisfaction.

During the pilot test, it's crucial to collect data on a variety of metrics to evaluate the tool's effectiveness. This could include the time saved, the accuracy of the tool's outputs, user satisfaction, and any changes in the quality of the work produced. It's also important to note any technical issues or challenges that arise, such as software bugs, difficulties in integration with other tools, or usability problems that could hinder adoption.

Once the pilot test is complete, a thorough review of the collected data and stakeholder feedback will provide a clearer picture of the tool's effectiveness and any potential issues. This is the time to engage with the vendor to discuss your findings, seek solutions to any problems, and possibly negotiate modifications or improvements to the tool. It's also an opportunity to decide whether to proceed with full-scale implementation, require further testing, or even to consider alternative solutions.

The insights gained from the pilot test can also inform training programs, helping to focus on areas where team members struggled or where the tool could be used more effectively. Moreover, the results can be used to build a business case for the full-scale implementation of the tool, providing evidence to support the investment in terms of time, money, and resources.

A pilot test is an essential step in the adoption of any new AI tool. It offers a low-risk way to evaluate the tool's effectiveness and identify any issues, providing the data and insights needed to make informed decisions about broader implementation.

Integration with Existing Systems

Ensuring seamless integration of new Artificial Intelligence (AI) tools with existing project management software and other systems is a critical step in the adoption process. The goal is to create a cohesive ecosystem where data flows smoothly between different platforms, and functionalities complement each other. This not only improves efficiency but also enhances the quality of project outcomes by enabling more informed decision-making.

The first step in this process is to conduct a thorough assessment of your existing software landscape. This involves understanding the functionalities of your current project management software, databases, communication platforms, and any other tools that are in use. Knowing the capabilities and limitations of these systems will help you identify what you need from the new AI tool and how it will fit into the existing setup.

Once you have a clear understanding of your existing systems, the next step is to define the specific integration requirements. This could range from data sharing and synchronization to more complex interactions like triggering workflows or automating specific tasks. At this stage, it's beneficial to consult with IT specialists and system architects to outline the technical specifications needed for integration. This could include API requirements, data formats, security protocols, and other technical details that will ensure a smooth integration process.

Engaging with the vendor of the AI tool is crucial at this point. A detailed discussion about your integration requirements will help you understand whether the tool is capable of meeting them. Some vendors offer custom integration services, which can be a valuable option if the tool doesn't natively support all the functionalities you need. It's also a good idea to ask for case studies or references from other organizations that have successfully integrated the tool with similar systems. This can provide valuable insights into the challenges and solutions that you might encounter.

Once the technical requirements are clear, and you have vendor support, the next step is to develop a detailed integration plan. This should outline the sequence of actions to be taken, responsible parties, and timelines. It's often advisable to start with a smaller-scale test integration before rolling it out fully. This allows you to identify any issues or bottlenecks in a controlled environment, making it easier to address them without disrupting ongoing projects.

During the integration process, continuous monitoring is essential. This involves tracking system performance, data accuracy, and user experience in real-time to quickly identify and address any issues. It's also important to have a rollback plan in place, allowing you to revert to the previous setup if the integration fails or causes significant problems.

After successful integration, it's crucial to train your team on how to use the new, integrated system effectively. This should include not just technical training but also guidelines on how to leverage the enhanced capabilities for better project outcomes. Regular feedback sessions with the team will help you understand how the integration is affecting day-to-day operations and whether any adjustments are needed.

Finally, integration is not a one-time task but an ongoing process. As both your existing systems and the new AI tool are updated or modified, you'll need to revisit the integration to ensure it remains seamless. This may require periodic reviews and adjustments to the integration architecture.

Integrating a new AI tool with existing project management software and other systems is a complex but crucial process. It requires careful planning, technical expertise, and ongoing monitoring to ensure that the tool not only fits into your existing software landscape but also enhances it, ultimately leading to more efficient and effective project management.

Monitoring and Feedback Loop

Establishing mechanisms for ongoing monitoring and feedback is a cornerstone for the successful implementation and sustained effectiveness of Artificial Intelligence (AI) tools in any project management environment. The dynamic nature of projects and the rapid advancements in AI technology make it imperative to have a system in place that can continually assess the tool's performance, user satisfaction, and overall impact on project outcomes.

The first step in establishing ongoing monitoring is to identify key performance indicators (KPIs) that will serve as measurable metrics for the AI tool's effectiveness. These could range from quantitative metrics like time saved, task completion rates, and error reduction to more qualitative measures like user satisfaction and the quality of project deliverables. The KPIs should align with the objectives that led to the adoption of the AI tool, whether that's improving efficiency, enhancing data analysis, or facilitating better communication among team members.

Once the KPIs are established, the next step is to set up the technical infrastructure needed for monitoring. This could involve integrating the AI tool with existing analytics platforms or setting up new dashboards specifically designed to track the tool's performance. Data collection should be automated to the extent possible to ensure that monitoring is continuous and not dependent on manual input. Security protocols must also be in place to protect the integrity and confidentiality of the data being collected.

In addition to automated data collection, it's important to have a system for gathering user feedback. This could be in the form of regular surveys, focus group discussions, or one-on-one interviews with team members and other stakeholders. User feedback provides valuable insights into the user experience, including any challenges faced in using the tool, and can help identify areas for improvement that may not be evident through quantitative metrics alone.

The collected data and feedback should be regularly reviewed by a cross-functional team comprising project managers, IT specialists, and possibly even representatives from the vendor of the AI tool. This team should meet at predetermined intervals—be it weekly, monthly, or quarterly—to analyze the data, discuss findings, and make recommendations for any adjustments or improvements. This is also an opportunity to review the KPIs themselves to ensure they remain relevant as project needs and technologies evolve.

Based on the findings from the ongoing monitoring, adjustments can be made to the AI tool's configurations, or additional training can be provided to users. In some cases, it may be necessary to consider switching to a different tool altogether if the current one is not meeting project objectives effectively. Any changes should be communicated clearly to all stakeholders and, if significant, may warrant a mini pilot test to ensure they achieve the desired outcomes.

Finally, the process of ongoing monitoring and feedback should be documented meticulously. This not only provides a historical record of performance but also facilitates future audits and serves as a valuable resource for other teams or departments considering the adoption of similar AI tools.

Ongoing monitoring and feedback are essential for maximizing the effectiveness of AI tools in project management. By setting clear KPIs, automating data collection, actively gathering user feedback, and regularly reviewing performance, organizations can ensure that their AI tools continue to add value to their projects and adapt to changing needs and technologies.

Section 5: Ethical and Legal Compliance

Data Privacy Measures

Ensuring compliance with data privacy laws such as the General Data Protection Regulation (GDPR) in Europe or the California Consumer Privacy Act (CCPA) in the United States is a critical aspect of implementing Artificial Intelligence (AI) tools in project management. These regulations have far-reaching implications for how personal data is collected, stored, and processed, and non-compliance can result in hefty fines and reputational damage.

The first step in ensuring compliance is to conduct a thorough review of the AI tool's data handling capabilities. This involves understanding what kind of data the tool will be collecting, how it will be stored, and what measures are in place to secure it. It's crucial to consult with legal experts who specialize in data privacy laws to get a clear understanding of your obligations under the relevant regulations. This legal advice should be integrated into a broader data governance strategy that outlines how data will be managed throughout its lifecycle.

Once you have a clear understanding of the legal landscape, the next step is to engage with the vendor of the AI tool to discuss compliance requirements. Many vendors offer features specifically designed to aid in compliance, such as data encryption, user access controls, and audit trails. However, it's important to not just rely on vendor claims and to conduct your own due diligence. This could involve a technical audit of the tool to ensure that it meets all the necessary security and privacy standards.

Data minimization is a key principle of many data privacy laws, meaning that you should only collect data that is strictly necessary for the purpose at hand. Therefore, it's important to configure the AI tool to limit data collection to what is essential for achieving your project objectives. This not only aids in compliance but also reduces the risk associated with potential data breaches.

Transparency is another important aspect of data privacy compliance. This means informing stakeholders, whether they are team members, clients, or end-users, about what data is being collected and how it will be used. Depending on the jurisdiction, you may be required to obtain explicit consent before collecting personal data. Therefore, clear communication and consent mechanisms should be in place before the AI tool is deployed.

Ongoing monitoring is essential to ensure continued compliance as both the regulatory environment and the AI tool itself evolve. This involves regular audits of data handling practices and security measures. Any changes to data privacy laws should be closely monitored, and the data governance strategy should be updated accordingly.

Training is another crucial element of compliance. All team members who will be interacting with the AI tool should be trained on data privacy best practices and the specific requirements of laws like GDPR or CCPA. This not only helps in ensuring compliance but also fosters a culture of data responsibility within the organization.

Ensuring that your AI tools comply with data privacy laws is a multi-faceted process that involves legal consultation, vendor engagement, technical audits, data minimization, transparency, ongoing monitoring, and training. By taking a proactive, informed approach, you can mitigate the risks associated with data privacy and ensure that your AI tools are both effective and compliant.

Ethical Guidelines

Developing ethical guidelines for the responsible use of Artificial Intelligence (AI) in projects is an imperative in today's increasingly data-driven world. These guidelines serve as a roadmap for project managers, team members, and stakeholders, ensuring that AI tools are used in a manner that is not only effective but also ethical. The guidelines should cover a range of issues, including but not limited to data bias and algorithmic fairness, to create a comprehensive framework for ethical AI use.

The first step in developing these guidelines is to assemble a cross-disciplinary team that includes not just project managers and AI experts, but also ethicists, legal advisors, and representatives from the communities that the project will impact. This ensures a diversity of perspectives, making the guidelines more robust and inclusive. The team should begin by identifying the ethical issues that are most relevant to the project. For example, if the project involves data analytics, issues related to data bias and algorithmic fairness will be of primary concern.

Once the key issues have been identified, the next step is to conduct a thorough review of existing ethical frameworks, best practices, and regulations related to AI. This provides a foundation upon which to build your guidelines and ensures that they are in line with current thinking in the field. It's also beneficial to consult with external experts and to review case studies of similar projects to understand how ethical challenges have been addressed in other contexts.

With this background research in hand, the team can begin drafting the guidelines. Each issue identified should be addressed in its own section, providing both a general overview of the ethical considerations and specific recommendations for responsible practice. For example, the section on data bias could discuss the importance of using diverse data sets to train algorithms and provide specific steps for auditing data for potential biases. Similarly, the section on algorithmic fairness could discuss the ethical implications of biased algorithms and provide guidelines for regular testing and validation to ensure that the algorithm's outputs are fair.

Transparency and accountability should be overarching themes in the guidelines. This means clearly documenting all decisions related to the use of AI, from the selection of data sets to the configuration of algorithms. It also means establishing mechanisms for accountability, such as regular ethical audits conducted by an independent body.

Once the draft guidelines are complete, they should be circulated among a wider group of stakeholders for feedback. This could include team members who will be using the AI tools, clients who will be impacted by the project, and even members of the public in cases where the project has broader societal implications. The feedback should be carefully reviewed and the guidelines revised accordingly.

After finalizing the guidelines, the next step is implementation. This involves integrating the guidelines into existing project management workflows and providing training to team members on ethical AI use. It's also important to establish ongoing monitoring mechanisms to ensure that the guidelines are being followed and to identify any ethical issues that arise during the course of the project.

Developing ethical guidelines for the responsible use of AI in projects is a complex but crucial task that involves multidisciplinary collaboration, thorough research, stakeholder consultation, and ongoing monitoring. By taking a proactive approach to ethical considerations, project managers can ensure that AI tools are used responsibly, effectively, and fairly, thereby enhancing the integrity and impact of their projects.

Section 6: Measuring ROI and Impact

Key Performance Indicators (KPIs)

Identifying Key Performance Indicators (KPIs) to measure the impact of Artificial Intelligence (AI) on project management is a critical step in assessing the value and effectiveness of AI tools. These KPIs serve as quantifiable metrics that can be tracked over time, providing a data-driven basis for decision-making and continuous improvement. The KPIs should be aligned with the specific objectives that led to the adoption of AI in the project, whether that's improving efficiency, enhancing data analysis, or facilitating better communication among team members.

One of the most straightforward KPIs to consider is time saved. AI tools can automate a variety of tasks, from data analysis to scheduling, freeing up team members to focus on more complex and creative aspects of the project. The time saved can be quantified in hours or days and translated into monetary terms based on average hourly rates for the team members involved. This provides a clear measure of the ROI (Return on Investment) for the AI tool in terms of time savings.

Cost reduction is another important KPI. AI tools can optimize resource allocation, reduce the need for rework by identifying errors early, and even predict potential risks that could lead to cost overruns. By tracking these metrics, you can quantify the cost savings achieved through the use of AI. It's important to factor in the cost of the AI tool itself, including not just the purchase price or subscription fee but also any costs associated with training and implementation, to get an accurate picture of the net cost reduction.

Improvement in stakeholder satisfaction is a more qualitative but equally important KPI. AI tools can enhance stakeholder engagement by providing more accurate and timely information, facilitating better communication, and even predicting stakeholder reactions based on historical data. Measuring stakeholder satisfaction can be done through regular surveys, interviews, or focus groups. While the results may be subjective, when tracked over time, they can provide valuable insights into the impact of AI on stakeholder relations.

Quality of project deliverables is another KPI that should not be overlooked. AI tools can improve the quality of deliverables by automating quality checks, providing advanced data analytics, or optimizing design processes. The quality can be measured using industry-specific metrics or through stakeholder feedback. An improvement in the quality of deliverables not only enhances stakeholder satisfaction but can also lead to long-term benefits such as increased customer loyalty or repeat business.

Risk mitigation is a more complex but highly valuable KPI. AI tools can analyze vast amounts of data to identify potential risks that might not be apparent through manual analysis. By tracking the number and severity of risks identified and mitigated through the use of AI, you can quantify its impact in terms of risk reduction.

Finally, it's important to consider KPIs related to the user experience of the team members who are interacting with the AI tool. This could include metrics related to the ease of use, the speed of task completion, and the rate of user adoption. A positive user experience not only facilitates the successful implementation of the AI tool but also contributes to its long-term effectiveness.

Identifying KPIs to measure the impact of AI on project management involves considering a range of factors, from time and cost savings to stakeholder satisfaction, quality of deliverables, risk mitigation, and user experience. These KPIs should be tracked regularly and analyzed to assess the effectiveness of the AI tool and to make data-driven decisions for continuous improvement.

Long-term Impact Assessment

While immediate Key Performance Indicators (KPIs) like time saved, cost reduction, and stakeholder satisfaction are essential for assessing the short-term impact of Artificial Intelligence (AI) on project management, it's equally important to consider the long-term impacts. These can be more subtle and may not manifest immediately, but they have the potential to significantly influence the project's success and the organization's overall competitiveness in the long run.

One such long-term impact is the enhancement of team skills. The introduction of AI tools often necessitates training and upskilling for team members. While this can be seen as a short-term investment in time and resources, the long-term benefits are considerable. Team members who are proficient in using advanced AI tools become more valuable assets to the organization. Their enhanced skills can lead to more innovative problem-solving and a higher quality of work, not just in the current project but in future initiatives as well. Over time, this upskilling can contribute to the organization's reputation as a leader in technological innovation, making it more attractive to both talent and clients.

Improved decision-making is another long-term impact that should not be underestimated. AI tools can analyze vast amounts of data more quickly and accurately than humans, providing insights that might not be apparent through manual analysis. As team members and project managers become more accustomed to incorporating these insights into their decision-making processes, the quality of decisions is likely to improve. Better decisions lead to better outcomes, whether that's choosing the most effective design for a product, selecting the best suppliers, or identifying the most promising market opportunities. Over time, this culture of data-driven decision-making can become a significant competitive advantage.

The potential for scaling the project is another long-term impact that can be influenced by the use of AI. Many AI tools are designed to be scalable, meaning they can handle larger volumes of data or more complex tasks as the project grows. This scalability can make it easier to expand the project or to replicate its success in different contexts. For example, an AI tool that has been successful in optimizing resource allocation in one project could potentially be applied to other projects within the organization, leading to company-wide efficiencies. Similarly, a machine learning algorithm that has proven effective in analyzing consumer behavior in one market could be adapted to other markets, accelerating the organization's global expansion efforts.

Moreover, the long-term data collected and analyzed by AI tools can become a valuable asset in itself. This data can be used for trend analysis, predictive modeling, and other advanced analytics, providing a foundation for strategic planning and long-term decision-making. It can also be leveraged for machine learning, allowing the AI tools to become more effective over time as they "learn" from the accumulated data.

While immediate KPIs provide important metrics for assessing the short-term impact of AI on project management, it's crucial to also consider the long-term impacts. These can include enhanced team skills, improved decision-making, and the potential for scaling the project, among others. By taking a holistic view that encompasses both the immediate and long-term impacts, project managers can make more informed decisions about the implementation of AI, maximizing its benefits for both the project and the organization as a whole.

Conclusion: The Road Ahead

Implementing AI in your project management practice is not a one-time effort but an ongoing journey. By carefully planning, selecting the right tools, training your team, and continuously monitoring and adapting, you can harness the full potential of AI to revolutionize your project management practice.

CHAPTER 9: CASE STUDIES: REAL-WORLD APPLICATIONS OF AI IN PROJECT MANAGEMENT

Introduction: The Proof is in the Practice

While theoretical discussions and guidelines provide valuable insights into the potential of AI in project management, nothing speaks louder than real-world applications. This chapter aims to delve into a series of case studies that showcase how organizations across various industries have successfully implemented AI in their project management practices.

Section 1: AI in Healthcare Project Management

Overview

Healthcare is an industry that stands at the intersection of human well-being and technological innovation. It's a sector fraught with complexities, from intricate medical procedures and protocols to stringent regulations that govern patient care and data handling. Given this complexity, the healthcare industry can benefit immensely from the capabilities of Artificial Intelligence (AI). This section delves into how a healthcare provider leveraged AI to improve project outcomes, offering a glimpse into the transformative potential of this technology.

The healthcare provider in question is a large hospital network with multiple locations. The organization was grappling with several challenges, including inefficiencies in patient scheduling, difficulties in resource allocation, and the need for more accurate diagnostics. Recognizing the potential of AI to address these issues, the hospital initiated a project to integrate AI technologies into its operations.

The first step was a comprehensive needs assessment to identify the specific areas where AI could have the most impact. After a series of consultations with medical professionals, administrative staff, and IT experts, the hospital decided to focus on three key areas: patient scheduling, resource allocation, and diagnostic accuracy.

For patient scheduling, the hospital implemented an AI-powered system that could predict patient flow based on historical data, seasonal trends, and other variables. This system was designed to optimize the use of medical facilities like operating rooms and imaging equipment, as well as to minimize patient wait times. The AI system used machine learning algorithms to continually refine its predictions, becoming more accurate over time. Within a few months of implementation, the hospital reported a significant reduction in patient wait times and a more efficient utilization of facilities.

Resource allocation was another critical area that was ripe for improvement. The hospital network had to manage a wide range of resources, from medical supplies to specialized personnel. An AI tool was developed to analyze various factors such as inventory levels, usage rates, and expiration dates for medical supplies, as well as staff schedules, skill sets, and workload for personnel. The tool could then recommend the most efficient allocation of these resources, leading to cost savings and improved patient care. For example, the system could predict when certain supplies were likely to run out and automatically place reorders, or it could suggest rescheduling staff to times when patient demand was expected to be high.

Improving diagnostic accuracy was the third focus area. The hospital implemented an AI system capable of analyzing medical images like X-rays and MRIs. Using deep learning algorithms, the system could identify patterns and anomalies that might be indicative of specific medical conditions. While not intended to replace human expertise, this tool served as an additional layer of analysis, helping medical professionals make more accurate diagnoses. Over time, the system was trained to recognize a broader range of conditions, becoming an invaluable aid in the diagnostic process.

The implementation of AI in these areas was not without challenges. The hospital had to navigate a complex regulatory landscape, ensuring that the AI tools were compliant with healthcare regulations, particularly those related to patient data privacy. Ethical considerations were also paramount, especially concerning the potential consequences of algorithmic errors in medical diagnoses. To address these concerns, the hospital established a robust governance framework and conducted regular audits of the AI systems.

The impact of the AI project was transformative. The hospital reported not only significant improvements in operational efficiency but also in the quality of patient care. The success of the project served as a catalyst for further innovation, encouraging the hospital to explore additional applications of AI in healthcare, from predictive analytics for patient outcomes to automated systems for monitoring patient vitals in real-time.

The healthcare provider's experience demonstrates the immense potential of AI to improve project outcomes in the complex and highly regulated healthcare industry. By carefully selecting focus areas, navigating regulatory and ethical considerations, and implementing robust AI solutions, the hospital was able to achieve significant improvements in efficiency, resource allocation, and diagnostic accuracy. This case serves as a compelling example of how AI can be effectively harnessed to address some of the most pressing challenges in healthcare today.

Case Study: Optimizing Hospital Resource Allocation

Introduction
The healthcare industry is a complex ecosystem where efficiency and effectiveness are not just buzzwords but critical factors that can impact human lives. In this intricate setting, a large hospital took a pioneering step by integrating machine learning algorithms to optimize the allocation of its medical staff and equipment. The initiative aimed to improve patient care while reducing operational costs. This case study explores the journey of this hospital, from the initial challenges to the successful outcomes achieved through the implementation of machine learning.

Background
The hospital in focus is a large, multi-specialty healthcare facility with a capacity of over 1,000 beds and a staff comprising various medical professionals, from surgeons and nurses to technicians and administrative personnel. The hospital was grappling with challenges related to inefficient resource allocation, including medical staff scheduling conflicts and underutilized medical equipment, which led to increased operational costs and compromised patient care.

The Challenge
The hospital's primary challenges were twofold:

- Medical Staff Allocation: Scheduling conflicts, overstaffing during low-demand periods, and understaffing during peak hours led to increased stress among medical staff and compromised patient care.
- Equipment Allocation: Expensive medical equipment like MRI machines, CT scanners, and surgical suites were often underutilized due to poor scheduling, leading to increased operational costs.

The Solution: Machine Learning Algorithms

Recognizing the need for a more efficient system, the hospital decided to implement machine learning algorithms to optimize resource allocation. A dedicated team of data scientists, healthcare professionals, and IT experts was formed to develop and implement the machine learning model.

The model was designed to analyze various data points, including historical patient inflow, staff availability, equipment usage rates, and even seasonal trends affecting healthcare demand. The algorithm would then predict the optimal allocation of medical staff and equipment for different time slots, aiming to maximize utilization while ensuring excellent patient care.

Implementation and Training

The machine learning model was initially trained on historical data, and its predictions were compared with actual outcomes to refine the algorithm. After several iterations, the model was integrated into the hospital's existing management software for real-time application. Staff members were trained on how to interact with the new system and interpret its recommendations.

Regulatory and Ethical Compliance

Given the sensitive nature of healthcare data, the hospital took extra precautions to ensure that the machine learning model complied with healthcare regulations, including data privacy laws. An ethics committee was also established to oversee the responsible use of machine learning in patient care.

Outcomes and Impact

The impact of the machine learning model was transformative:

- Improved Patient Care: Optimized staff allocation led to reduced wait times and better patient outcomes. The model could even predict spikes in demand, allowing the hospital to allocate additional resources proactively.
- Reduced Costs: Efficient equipment scheduling led to higher utilization rates, significantly reducing operational costs. The hospital reported a 20% reduction in costs related to resource allocation within the first year of implementation.
- Staff Satisfaction: The elimination of scheduling conflicts and the more rational distribution of workload led to increased job satisfaction among the medical staff.

Lessons Learned and Future Directions

While the project was a resounding success, it was not without challenges. Data quality and integrity were ongoing concerns, and the hospital had to invest in regular audits and updates to the machine learning model. Additionally, the human element—convincing staff to trust and act on the algorithm's recommendations—required focused change management efforts.

The hospital plans to extend the use of machine learning to other areas, such as predictive diagnostics and personalized treatment plans, building on the success of this project.

Conclusion

This case study serves as a compelling example of how machine learning can revolutionize resource allocation in a large healthcare setting. By leveraging advanced algorithms, the hospital was able to significantly improve patient care while reducing operational costs, setting a precedent for other healthcare institutions to follow.

Lessons Learned

Data Quality: The importance of high-quality, accurate data for training the machine learning model.

Stakeholder Buy-in: How the project team secured buy-in from medical staff through transparent communication and training.

Section 2: AI in Software Development Projects

Overview

Software development projects are a hotbed of complexity and dynamism. They often involve multiple teams working in tandem, each with its own set of tasks, timelines, and deliverables. Add to this the ever-changing requirements that can shift due to client needs, market trends, or technological advancements, and you have a landscape that is anything but static. Tight deadlines further compound these challenges, leaving project managers in a constant struggle to balance quality, scope, time, and cost. In such a volatile environment, Artificial Intelligence (AI) emerges as a game-changing ally that can offer significant advantages in managing these multifaceted challenges.

One of the most immediate benefits of AI in software development projects is its ability to automate routine and repetitive tasks. From code generation to bug tracking and even preliminary testing, AI algorithms can handle a range of activities that would otherwise consume a developer's time. This automation not only speeds up the development process but also frees up human resources to focus on more complex and creative aspects of the project, such as architectural design or problem-solving.

Beyond automation, AI brings the power of predictive analytics to the table. By analyzing historical data from past projects, machine learning algorithms can forecast potential roadblocks or delays in the project timeline. These predictive insights enable project managers to take proactive measures, such as reallocating resources or revising schedules, well before a problem turns into a crisis. This kind of foresight is invaluable in an industry where delays can result in significant financial losses and damage to reputation.

AI also excels in resource allocation, one of the most challenging aspects of project management. Machine learning algorithms can analyze a multitude of variables, such as team members' skills, past performance, and current workload, to recommend the most efficient allocation of human and material resources. This level of optimization is often beyond the capacity of even the most experienced project managers, who may have to rely on gut feeling or incomplete information.

Another area where AI can make a substantial impact is stakeholder communication. Natural Language Processing (NLP) algorithms can analyze written or spoken communication to gauge the sentiment and priorities of clients or team members. This data-driven approach can guide project managers in tailoring their communication and negotiation strategies, ensuring that stakeholder expectations are managed effectively.

Quality assurance is yet another domain ripe for AI intervention. Traditional testing methods, although reliable, are often time-consuming and may not cover all potential scenarios where a software could fail. AI-driven testing tools can simulate a variety of conditions to identify vulnerabilities or performance issues that might not surface under standard testing protocols. This ensures a more robust final product and can significantly reduce the time and cost associated with post-launch fixes.

Moreover, AI's role is not just limited to the development phase; it extends into the maintenance and improvement stages as well. Post-launch, AI tools can monitor user behavior and feedback to identify areas for improvement or even suggest new features that could enhance the product's market fit.

The integration of AI into software development projects offers a multi-dimensional array of benefits. From automating mundane tasks and optimizing resource allocation to predictive analytics and enhanced quality assurance, AI has the potential to revolutionize the way software projects are managed. By mitigating risks, reducing costs, and improving efficiency, AI empowers project managers and developers alike to navigate the complexities of modern software development with unprecedented agility and insight.

Case Study: Predictive Analytics for Bug Tracking

Introduction
In the fast-paced world of software development, quality assurance (QA) is often a bottleneck that can delay releases and escalate costs. Traditional QA methods, although effective, can be time-consuming and reactive rather than proactive. This case study delves into how a leading software development company leveraged predictive analytics to forecast potential bugs and vulnerabilities, thereby enabling proactive quality assurance measures that significantly improved the software's reliability and reduced time-to-market.

Background
The company in focus is a well-established software development firm specializing in enterprise solutions. With a diverse clientele and a broad range of projects, the company was facing increasing challenges in maintaining high-quality software releases. The traditional QA methods, involving manual testing and code reviews, were becoming increasingly inadequate in handling the complexity and scale of their projects.

The Challenge
The primary challenge was twofold:

Time-Consuming QA Process: The existing QA methods were labor-intensive and time-consuming, often delaying the project timelines.

Reactive Rather Than Proactive: The traditional QA approach was inherently reactive, identifying bugs and vulnerabilities only after they had been coded, requiring costly and time-consuming revisions.

The Solution: Predictive Analytics

To address these challenges, the company decided to implement predictive analytics into their QA process. They developed a machine learning model trained on historical data from past projects, including bug reports, code changes, and developer notes. The model was designed to predict the likelihood of bugs or vulnerabilities based on various factors such as code complexity, development stage, and even the individual developer's historical performance.

Implementation and Training

The predictive analytics model was integrated into the company's existing development environment. Developers were trained on how to interpret the model's predictions and take proactive measures. For example, if the model predicted a high likelihood of bugs in a particular module, developers would prioritize that module for more intensive testing or even redesign.

Regulatory and Ethical Compliance

Given that the software often dealt with sensitive enterprise data, the predictive analytics model was designed to be compliant with data privacy and security regulations. The company also ensured that the model's predictions were used as guidelines rather than absolute measures to avoid any ethical concerns related to developer performance evaluation.

Outcomes and Impact

The implementation of predictive analytics had a transformative impact on the company's QA process:

- Reduced Time-to-Market: By identifying potential issues early in the development cycle, the company was able to reduce the overall time spent on QA, accelerating the time-to-market for their products.
- Cost Savings: Proactive identification and resolution of bugs reduced the costs associated with late-stage revisions and post-launch patches.
- Improved Software Quality: The predictive model helped the team focus their QA efforts more effectively, resulting in a more reliable final product.

Lessons Learned and Future Directions

The project was not without its challenges. The quality and consistency of historical data were significant concerns, and the company had to invest in data cleaning and normalization. There was also initial resistance from developers who were skeptical about the model's accuracy. However, as the model proved its effectiveness over time, it gained wider acceptance.

The company plans to refine the model further by incorporating real-time data and possibly extending its capabilities to predict other aspects of software development, such as time estimates for task completion.

Conclusion

This case study demonstrates the transformative potential of predictive analytics in software development, particularly in the realm of quality assurance. By shifting from a reactive to a proactive approach, the company not only improved the quality of its software products but also achieved significant cost savings and efficiency gains. The experience offers valuable insights for other software development firms looking to innovate their QA processes.

Lessons Learned

Agile Integration: How AI was integrated into the company's Agile methodology.

Continuous Improvement: The role of ongoing data analysis in refining the predictive model.

Section 3: AI in Construction Project Management

Overview

Construction projects are inherently complex endeavors that require the orchestration of a multitude of variables. These variables range from the tangible, such as material and labor costs, to the unpredictable, like weather conditions. Each of these elements can significantly impact the project's timeline, budget, and overall success. Given this complexity, construction projects are ideal candidates for optimization through Artificial Intelligence (AI).

In the realm of material and labor costs, AI can offer invaluable insights. Traditional methods of cost estimation often rely on historical data and human expertise, which, while valuable, can be subject to errors and limitations. AI algorithms can analyze vast datasets that include not just historical cost information but also real-time market prices for materials and labor rates. By doing so, they can provide more accurate and dynamic cost estimations. This level of detail allows project managers to budget more effectively, reducing the likelihood of cost overruns that are all too common in the construction industry.

Weather conditions are another critical variable in construction projects. Adverse weather can delay tasks, damage materials, and even pose safety risks to workers. While no one can control the weather, AI can help project managers plan for it. Predictive analytics can analyze years of weather data in the project's location to forecast likely weather conditions during the project timeline. This information can guide decisions about when to schedule weather-sensitive tasks or when to order weather-sensitive materials. In doing so, AI helps in mitigating the risks and delays associated with weather unpredictability.

AI's capabilities extend beyond these examples. For instance, machine learning algorithms can analyze past projects to identify potential bottlenecks or inefficiencies in a new project's plan. Natural Language Processing (NLP) can be used to analyze contractual documents, identifying terms or clauses that could pose risks down the line. Computer vision algorithms can analyze drone-captured images of the construction site, providing real-time updates on progress and flagging any discrepancies between the plan and the actual construction.

In essence, the multifaceted nature of construction projects makes them ripe for AI-driven optimization. By analyzing and learning from both historical and real-time data, AI can provide project managers with actionable insights across a project's lifecycle. Whether it's more accurate cost estimations, weather forecasts, or real-time monitoring of construction progress, AI has the potential to make construction projects more efficient, cost-effective, and less risky. The integration of AI into construction project management is not just a technological advancement; it's a paradigm shift that could redefine how the construction industry operates.

Case Study: Drone Surveillance for Real-time Monitoring

Introduction

The construction industry has long been plagued by inefficiencies, cost overruns, and delays, often due to the lack of real-time, accurate data for monitoring progress. This case study explores how a leading construction company leveraged AI-powered drones to revolutionize its approach to real-time monitoring of construction sites. The result was not only more accurate progress tracking but also the early identification of potential issues that could derail the project.

Background

The construction company in focus is a large-scale firm specializing in commercial and residential buildings. With projects often spanning several acres and involving hundreds of workers, the company faced significant challenges in monitoring construction progress. Traditional methods, such as manual inspections and reports, were time-consuming and often failed to capture the full scope of a project's status.

The Challenge

The primary challenges were:

- Lack of Real-Time Data: Traditional monitoring methods provided only periodic updates, making it difficult to react quickly to issues as they arose.
- Inaccurate Progress Tracking: Manual methods were prone to human error, leading to inaccuracies that could affect project timelines and budgets.
- Early Identification of Issues: Without real-time data, potential problems like structural issues or delays in material delivery were often identified too late for preventive action.

The Solution: AI-Powered Drones

To address these challenges, the company decided to deploy drones equipped with advanced AI algorithms and computer vision capabilities. These drones would fly over the construction sites at regular intervals, capturing high-resolution images and videos. The AI algorithms would then analyze this data in real-time to assess construction progress, identify discrepancies between the planned and actual construction, and flag potential issues such as safety hazards.

Implementation

After a pilot phase to test the technology's reliability and accuracy, the drones were deployed across multiple construction sites. The AI algorithms were trained to recognize various construction elements like walls, beams, and machinery, and to compare the real-time data against the construction plans. The system was integrated with the company's existing project management software, allowing for seamless communication between the drones' monitoring capabilities and the project managers.

Regulatory and Safety Compliance

Given the potential risks associated with drone flights, the company ensured that the drones complied with all relevant safety and aviation regulations. Flight paths were carefully planned to minimize disruption and risks to workers on the site.

Outcomes and Impact

The impact of implementing AI-powered drones was transformative:

- Real-Time Monitoring: The drones provided real-time data, enabling immediate action to address issues, thereby reducing delays and cost overruns.
- Accurate Progress Tracking: The AI algorithms ensured a high level of accuracy in tracking construction progress, leading to more effective project management.
- Early Identification of Issues: The system was effective in flagging potential problems early, allowing for preventive measures that saved both time and money.

Lessons Learned and Future Directions

While the implementation was largely successful, there were challenges such as initial resistance from on-site workers concerned about job displacement and privacy. However, through training and demonstration of the drones' effectiveness, these concerns were largely mitigated.

The company plans to further refine the AI algorithms to include predictive analytics for even earlier identification of potential issues. They are also exploring the integration of additional sensors on the drones to monitor environmental conditions like temperature and humidity, which could affect construction materials.

Conclusion

This case study demonstrates the transformative potential of AI-powered drones in the construction industry. By enabling real-time, accurate monitoring, the technology helped the company overcome traditional challenges in project management, leading to more efficient and cost-effective construction processes. The experience offers valuable insights for other construction firms looking to leverage advanced technology to improve project outcomes.

Lessons Learned

Regulatory Compliance: Navigating the legal landscape around drone usage.

Data Integration: How the drone data was integrated into the overall project management system.

Section 4: AI in Marketing and Customer Engagement Projects

Overview

In the fast-paced world of marketing, the ability to stay ahead of consumer trends is not just an advantage; it's a necessity. Traditional methods of understanding consumer behavior often involve time-consuming processes like focus groups, surveys, or manual data analysis, which can offer valuable insights but also come with their limitations. These methods are often reactive, providing a snapshot of consumer sentiment that may already be outdated by the time the data is analyzed and actionable insights are generated.

Enter Artificial Intelligence, a game-changer in the realm of marketing. AI has the capability to analyze vast amounts of data in real-time, offering insights that are both immediate and highly relevant. For instance, machine learning algorithms can sift through social media posts, online reviews, and even video content to gauge consumer sentiment about a brand or product. This real-time analysis allows marketers to understand not just what consumers are thinking but also why they are thinking it, providing a depth of understanding that was previously unattainable.

But AI goes beyond just understanding current consumer behavior; it can also predict future behavior. Predictive analytics can analyze past purchasing behavior, click-through rates, and even how long a consumer spends looking at a particular product online to predict future purchases. This enables marketers to tailor their strategies to individual consumer preferences, enhancing the personalization of marketing efforts. In an age where consumers are bombarded with information and choices, this level of personalization can make the difference between a consumer choosing your product over a competitor's.

AI can also revolutionize content marketing by analyzing which types of content resonate most with target audiences. Natural Language Processing (NLP) can evaluate the language style, tone, and structure that are most engaging for specific consumer groups, allowing for the creation of highly targeted and effective content. Similarly, computer vision algorithms can analyze visual content to determine what types of images or videos are most appealing to consumers.

Moreover, AI's data-driven insights can be integrated seamlessly into a company's existing marketing strategy. This allows for a more agile approach to marketing, where strategies can be adapted in real-time as consumer preferences evolve. This is particularly crucial in today's digital age, where trends can change in the blink of an eye and yesterday's marketing strategies can quickly become obsolete.

AI offers a transformative approach to understanding and predicting consumer behavior in the fast-paced world of marketing. Its ability to analyze large datasets in real-time provides marketers with immediate, actionable insights that can be integrated into an agile, responsive marketing strategy. By offering a deeper understanding of consumer preferences and the ability to predict future behavior, AI enables marketers to stay ahead of trends, offering a significant competitive advantage in an increasingly crowded marketplace.

Case Study: Sentiment Analysis for Campaign Optimization

Introduction

In the ever-evolving landscape of digital marketing, the ability to adapt and pivot is crucial. Traditional metrics like click-through rates and conversion rates are valuable, but they often don't tell the whole story. This case study delves into how a cutting-edge marketing agency used sentiment analysis, powered by Artificial Intelligence, to gauge the effectiveness of various marketing campaigns in real-time. This innovative approach allowed for immediate adjustments, optimizing the campaigns and delivering unparalleled results for their clients.

Background

The marketing agency in question is a mid-sized firm specializing in digital campaigns for consumer goods companies. They have a diverse clientele, ranging from startups to Fortune 500 companies.

Despite their success, they faced challenges in assessing the emotional impact of their campaigns on consumers. Traditional metrics could quantify engagement but couldn't measure sentiment, a key indicator of brand perception and customer loyalty.

The Challenge

The agency needed to answer several pressing questions:

- How are consumers emotionally reacting to different campaigns?
- Which elements of the campaigns are resonating positively or negatively?
- Can real-time adjustments be made to optimize ongoing campaigns?

The Solution: Sentiment Analysis Powered by AI

To address these challenges, the agency turned to sentiment analysis algorithms capable of interpreting consumer reactions across various platforms, including social media, online forums, and customer reviews. These algorithms were designed to understand the nuances of human emotion, categorizing sentiments as positive, negative, or neutral. They could also identify specific emotional triggers within the content, such as joy, surprise, or anger.

Implementation

After a brief pilot phase, the agency integrated the sentiment analysis tool into their existing analytics dashboard. The tool continuously monitored consumer reactions to different campaigns, providing real-time updates. It was also capable of segmenting the data based on demographics, geographical location, and other variables, offering a multi-dimensional view of consumer sentiment.

Real-Time Adjustments

One of the most groundbreaking aspects of this approach was the ability to make real-time adjustments to ongoing campaigns. For instance, if the sentiment analysis tool detected a negative reaction to a particular ad, the agency could immediately pause that ad and investigate the cause of the negative sentiment. This allowed for quick course corrections, saving both time and money.

Outcomes and Impact

The results were nothing short of transformative:

- Enhanced Campaign Effectiveness: The agency reported a significant increase in the effectiveness of their campaigns, including higher engagement rates and improved ROI.
- Client Satisfaction: Clients were thrilled with the ability to understand consumer sentiment in real-time, leading to more long-term contracts for the agency.
- Brand Perception: By avoiding negative sentiment and amplifying positive reactions, the agency was able to significantly improve the brand perception of their clients.

Lessons Learned and Future Directions

While the sentiment analysis tool was highly effective, it was not without its challenges. The agency had to invest in training their staff to interpret the data correctly and make informed decisions. They also found that sentiment analysis was most effective when used in conjunction with traditional metrics, providing a more holistic view of campaign effectiveness.

Looking ahead, the agency plans to explore more advanced AI techniques, such as predictive analytics, to forecast consumer sentiment and preemptively adjust campaigns. They are also considering expanding the use of sentiment analysis to other areas, such as product development and customer service.

Conclusion

This case study demonstrates the immense potential of using AI-powered sentiment analysis in digital marketing. By understanding consumer sentiment in real-time, the agency was able to make immediate adjustments to their campaigns, leading to improved effectiveness and client satisfaction. This innovative approach offers valuable insights for any marketing firm looking to gain a competitive edge in today's digital landscape.

Lessons Learned

Data Privacy: Ensuring compliance with data privacy regulations while analyzing customer data.

Stakeholder Communication: How the insights from sentiment analysis were communicated to clients and stakeholders.

Section 5: AI in Supply Chain and Logistics Projects

Overview

Supply chain and logistics form the backbone of many industries, from manufacturing and retail to healthcare and food services. Traditionally, these areas have been managed using a combination of manual oversight and basic software tools, which, while effective, often lack the flexibility and real-time analytics needed to adapt to rapidly changing conditions. The advent of Artificial Intelligence has the potential to revolutionize these critical aspects of business operations, offering a level of optimization previously unattainable.

One of the most immediate impacts of AI in supply chain management is in the area of predictive analytics. By analyzing historical data and current trends, AI algorithms can forecast future demand for products with a high degree of accuracy. This enables companies to adjust their production schedules, manage inventory levels, and even negotiate better terms with suppliers. The end result is a more efficient supply chain with lower costs and faster delivery times.

In logistics, AI can optimize routing for transportation, taking into account a multitude of variables such as traffic conditions, weather forecasts, and fuel costs. This is particularly crucial for industries that rely on the timely delivery of perishable goods or high-value items. AI algorithms can dynamically adjust routes in real-time, ensuring that goods are delivered in the most efficient manner possible, thereby reducing costs and improving customer satisfaction.

AI can also play a significant role in quality control within the supply chain. Computer vision algorithms can inspect products on a manufacturing line, identifying defects or inconsistencies much faster and more accurately than a human inspector. This not only improves the quality of the end product but also reduces waste and lowers the risk of costly recalls or customer complaints.

Moreover, AI can enhance supplier relationship management by analyzing performance metrics and contractual compliance, thereby identifying opportunities for renegotiation or process improvement.

This is particularly valuable in complex supply chains that involve multiple suppliers across different geographical locations, where manual oversight would be both time-consuming and error-prone.

Another area where AI is making inroads is in the automation of warehouse operations. Robots, guided by AI algorithms, can sort, pick, and pack products far more efficiently than human workers. This not only speeds up the order fulfillment process but also reduces the risk of workplace accidents.

However, the implementation of AI in supply chain and logistics is not without its challenges. Data privacy and security are of paramount importance, especially when AI algorithms are analyzing sensitive business information. Companies must also invest in training their staff to work alongside AI tools, ensuring that human expertise and machine intelligence are effectively integrated.

Despite these challenges, the benefits of AI in supply chain and logistics are too significant to ignore. From predictive analytics and route optimization to quality control and automated warehousing, AI offers a range of solutions that can drastically improve operational efficiency. As AI technology continues to advance, it's likely that its role in supply chain and logistics will only grow, offering even more opportunities for optimization and innovation.

Case Study: Real-time Inventory Management

Introduction

Inventory management has always been a critical aspect of retail operations, affecting everything from storage costs to customer satisfaction. Traditional inventory systems, while functional, often lack the real-time analytics needed to adapt to fast-changing consumer demands. This case study examines how a leading retail company leveraged Artificial Intelligence algorithms for real-time inventory management, resulting in significant reductions in storage costs and improvements in service levels.

Background

The retail company in focus is a well-known brand with hundreds of stores across the country, offering a wide range of consumer goods. Despite its market leadership, the company faced challenges in managing its complex inventory system, which included multiple suppliers, seasonal fluctuations in demand, and the need for rapid restocking of popular items.

The Challenge

The company's existing inventory management system was largely manual, relying on periodic audits and static formulas to determine stock levels. This approach led to several issues:

- Overstocking of less popular items, resulting in high storage costs.
- Understocking of in-demand products, leading to lost sales and customer dissatisfaction.
- Inefficiencies in warehouse operations, including wasted man-hours in stock verification and reordering.

The Solution: Real-Time Inventory Management Powered by AI

To address these challenges, the company decided to implement an AI-powered inventory management system capable of real-time analytics. The system used machine learning algorithms to analyze historical sales data, current stock levels, and other relevant factors like seasonal trends and promotional events. Based on this analysis, the system could predict future demand for each product with high accuracy and adjust stock levels in real-time.

Implementation

After a successful pilot program in a few select stores, the AI-powered inventory system was rolled out across all locations. The system was integrated with the company's existing ERP software, ensuring a seamless transition. Real-time dashboards were set up to monitor stock levels, demand forecasts, and other key metrics, accessible to both store managers and central inventory planners.

Outcomes and Impact

The impact of the new system was immediate and substantial:

- Reduced Storage Costs: By optimizing stock levels, the company was able to reduce its storage costs by 20% within the first year of implementation.
- Improved Service Levels: Real-time adjustments to inventory meant that popular items were always in stock, leading to a 15% increase in customer satisfaction ratings.
- Operational Efficiency: The system automated many of the manual tasks associated with inventory management, freeing up staff to focus on customer service and other value-added activities.

Lessons Learned and Future Directions

The implementation process was not without its challenges. Staff had to be trained to interpret and act upon the real-time data provided by the system. Additionally, the machine learning algorithms required a few months of data collection to 'learn' and become fully effective.

Going forward, the company plans to integrate the AI inventory system with its online retail platform, enabling even more precise demand forecasting. They are also exploring the use of AI in other areas of operations, such as customer service and supply chain management.

Conclusion

This case study demonstrates the transformative potential of AI in retail inventory management. By adopting a real-time, data-driven approach, the company was able to significantly reduce costs, improve service levels, and enhance operational efficiency. The experience serves as a valuable lesson for other retail companies looking to modernize their inventory systems and gain a competitive edge in today's fast-paced market.

Lessons Learned

Scalability: How the AI system was designed to scale with the growing needs of the business.

Cross-functional Collaboration: The importance of collaboration between the project team and other departments like sales and operations.

Conclusion: The Transformative Power of AI in Practice

The case studies in this chapter demonstrate the transformative power of AI across various industries and types of projects. They serve as both inspiration and a practical guide for project managers looking to implement AI in their own practices.

CHAPTER 10: CONCLUSION AND FUTURE OUTLOOK: NAVIGATING THE AI-DRIVEN TRANSFORMATION IN PROJECT MANAGEMENT

Introduction: The Dawn of a New Era

As we've explored throughout this book, the integration of Artificial Intelligence into the realm of project management is not merely a trend—it's a transformative shift that is reshaping the industry. This concluding chapter aims to summarize the key takeaways and provide a roadmap for navigating the AI-driven transformation in project management.

Section 1: Key Takeaways

The Multifaceted Impact of AI

Artificial Intelligence (AI) has been heralded as a transformative force across industries, and project management is no exception. However, it's crucial to understand that AI is not a panacea that will solve all project management challenges. Rather, it's a versatile tool with a broad range of applications that can significantly enhance different facets of project management.

When it comes to data analysis and decision-making, AI offers unparalleled advantages. Traditional methods often involve manual sorting through data, which is not only time-consuming but also susceptible to human error. AI, particularly machine learning algorithms, can quickly analyze large datasets, identifying patterns and trends that might be difficult or even impossible for a human to discern. This rapid, automated analysis can be a game-changer for project managers, providing them with timely and accurate insights that can inform crucial decisions. For example, AI can sift through historical project data to identify potential risks, enabling project managers to take proactive measures to mitigate those risks.

In the realm of team collaboration, AI has the potential to revolutionize the way teams communicate and work together. Intelligent communication platforms, powered by AI algorithms, can prioritize and filter messages, suggest the best times for team meetings, and even offer real-time translation services for globally dispersed teams. These capabilities can significantly streamline communication processes, ensuring that everyone is aligned and reducing the chances of misunderstandings that can derail projects. AI can also integrate with existing project management software to automate routine tasks, flag issues that require immediate attention, and even suggest optimal task assignments based on team members' skills and current workload.

Stakeholder engagement is another critical area where AI can make a significant impact. Managing stakeholder expectations and communications is a complex task, especially in large projects with multiple stakeholders. AI, particularly Natural Language Processing (NLP) algorithms, can analyze various forms of stakeholder communications to gauge sentiment and attitudes. This data-driven approach can provide project managers with invaluable insights into stakeholder concerns, enabling them to proactively address issues and manage expectations more effectively.

However, it's essential to note that the effectiveness of AI in project management is not uniform; it varies depending on the specific needs and constraints of each project. Therefore, project managers need to assess which AI tools and algorithms are most relevant for their projects carefully. This often involves a period of customization and fine-tuning to ensure that the AI tools are aligned with the project's objectives and requirements.

Moreover, as AI systems become more integrated into project management processes, ethical and legal considerations come to the forefront. Issues such as data privacy, algorithmic fairness, and compliance with regulations become increasingly important. Project managers, therefore, must be vigilant in ensuring that their AI tools are both ethical and compliant with relevant laws, especially when these tools are used to analyze sensitive or personal data.

While AI is not a one-size-fits-all solution, it is a highly adaptable and powerful tool that can significantly improve various aspects of project management. From enhancing data analysis and decision-making to facilitating better team collaboration and stakeholder engagement, the potential benefits are vast. However, these benefits can only be fully realized if project managers approach AI as a flexible tool that needs to be carefully tailored to fit the specific needs and ethical considerations of each project.

Ethical and Legal Imperatives

The integration of Artificial Intelligence into project management is not just a matter of technological innovation but also brings with it a host of ethical and legal considerations that project managers must be prepared to address. As AI systems become more sophisticated and their applications more varied, the ethical and legal landscape surrounding their use becomes increasingly complex.

One of the most pressing issues is that of data privacy. AI systems often require access to vast amounts of data to function effectively. This data can include sensitive information about stakeholders, employees, or customers. The collection, storage, and analysis of this data must be conducted in a manner that respects individual privacy rights and complies with relevant laws, such as the General Data Protection Regulation (GDPR) in Europe or the California Consumer Privacy Act (CCPA) in the United States. Project managers must be aware of these regulations and ensure that any AI tools used in their projects are compliant. This may involve conducting privacy impact assessments, implementing robust data encryption methods, and ensuring that data is anonymized when used for training AI models.

Algorithmic fairness is another critical ethical consideration. AI algorithms can inadvertently perpetuate or even exacerbate existing biases in society, leading to unfair or discriminatory outcomes. For instance, an AI tool used for resource allocation could inadvertently favor one group over another based on biased historical data. Project managers must be vigilant in ensuring that AI tools are designed and deployed in a manner that minimizes bias. This could involve using diverse training data, regularly reviewing algorithms to identify and rectify any biases, and even consulting with ethicists or other experts in the field to ensure that the AI system's decision-making processes are as fair and unbiased as possible.

Transparency and accountability are also significant concerns. As AI systems take on more decision-making roles in projects, there needs to be a clear understanding of how these decisions are made. The emerging field of Explainable AI (XAI) aims to make the decision-making processes of AI algorithms understandable to humans, which is crucial for building trust and ensuring accountability. Project managers should prioritize the use of AI systems that provide a level of transparency in their operations and should be prepared to explain these operations to stakeholders.

Legal considerations are closely tied to these ethical concerns. As AI systems become more autonomous, questions arise about legal responsibility for their actions. For example, if an AI system makes a decision that leads to financial loss or harm, who is held accountable? Is it the project manager, the organization, or the developers of the AI system? Legal frameworks for AI are still in their infancy, and project managers must stay abreast of ongoing developments in this area to mitigate risks.

As AI becomes more deeply integrated into the field of project management, ethical and legal considerations will take on heightened importance. Project managers will need to navigate a complex landscape of data privacy regulations, ethical considerations around algorithmic fairness, and emerging legal frameworks. Proactive engagement with these issues is not just a matter of compliance but is crucial for building trust and ensuring the responsible use of AI in project management.

The Importance of Adaptability

The landscape of Artificial Intelligence is akin to shifting sands, constantly changing and evolving with each technological breakthrough and each new piece of research. For project managers, this dynamic environment presents both an opportunity and a challenge. The opportunity lies in the potential to leverage increasingly sophisticated AI tools to enhance various aspects of project management, from data analysis and decision-making to team collaboration and stakeholder engagement. The challenge, however, is in keeping up with this fast-paced evolution and ensuring that one's skills and methodologies are up-to-date.

Adaptability is no longer just a desirable trait for project managers; it's a necessity. As AI technologies become more advanced, the tools that were considered state-of-the-art just a few years ago may quickly become obsolete. Project managers must be willing to continually update their skills to understand not just the basics of AI but also more advanced concepts like machine learning, natural language processing, and even quantum computing. This may involve taking specialized courses, attending workshops, or even going back to school for more formal education. The goal is not necessarily to become an AI expert but to have enough understanding to effectively collaborate with specialists and to make informed decisions about the use of AI in projects.

Methodologies in project management, too, will need to evolve to incorporate AI capabilities. Traditional methodologies may not be equipped to handle the real-time data analysis, automated decision-making, and other dynamic elements that AI can introduce into a project. As methodologies like Agile and DevOps become more prevalent, AI can play a crucial role in automating routine tasks and providing real-time insights, making these approaches even more efficient. Project managers will need to be familiar with how AI tools can fit into different methodologies and be willing to adapt or even overhaul their existing processes to take full advantage of AI capabilities.

Moreover, the integration of AI into project management is not just about leveraging new tools but also about fostering a culture of continuous improvement and learning within the team. As AI systems become more integrated into project workflows, team members will also need to update their skills and adapt to new ways of working. Project managers will play a crucial role in facilitating this cultural shift, providing the necessary training and resources and creating an environment where team members feel empowered to innovate and experiment.

Another aspect to consider is the ethical and legal landscape surrounding AI, which is also continually evolving. Project managers will need to stay abreast of new regulations and ethical guidelines that may affect the use of AI in their projects. This will require not just ongoing education but also a willingness to engage with complex ethical and legal issues proactively.

The ever-evolving landscape of AI presents both exciting opportunities and formidable challenges for project managers. To navigate this landscape successfully, project managers will need to be adaptable, continually updating their skills and methodologies to leverage the latest advancements in AI. This will involve a commitment to lifelong learning, a willingness to adapt existing processes, and the ability to foster a culture of innovation and continuous improvement within their teams. Only by doing so can project managers hope to fully harness the transformative power of AI in the field of project management.

Section 2: Practical Steps for Project Managers

Continuous Learning and Skill Development

The rapid pace of advancements in Artificial Intelligence (AI) technology and methodology necessitates a commitment to continuous learning for project managers. Gone are the days when a project manager could rely solely on traditional management techniques and tools. As AI becomes increasingly integrated into various aspects of project management, from data analytics and risk assessment to resource allocation and stakeholder engagement, staying current with the latest developments becomes not just advantageous but essential.

Continuous learning in the context of AI for project management is multi-faceted. First and foremost, it involves keeping up-to-date with the latest technological advancements. AI is a field that is continually evolving, with new algorithms, tools, and applications emerging regularly. Project managers don't need to become AI experts, but they do need a solid understanding of the capabilities and limitations of current AI technologies. This knowledge enables them to make informed decisions about which AI tools to implement in their projects and how to use them effectively. It also allows them to communicate more effectively with AI specialists, facilitating better collaboration and ultimately leading to more successful project outcomes.

But it's not just about understanding the technology; it's also about understanding how to apply it within the specific context of project management. This means staying abreast of new methodologies and best practices for integrating AI into various project management tasks and workflows. As AI technology evolves, so too do the methodologies for applying it. What was considered a best practice a year ago may now be outdated, replaced by more effective techniques and approaches. Project managers need to be aware of these shifts and be prepared to adapt their methods accordingly.

Continuous learning also extends to the ethical and legal dimensions of using AI in project management. As society grapples with the broader implications of AI, new regulations and ethical guidelines are likely to emerge that will impact how AI can be used in a project management context. Project managers must stay informed about these developments to ensure that their use of AI is both legally compliant and ethically responsible.

So how can project managers invest in continuous learning? There are multiple avenues to explore:

1. Formal Education: Many educational institutions offer courses on AI and machine learning, ranging from introductory classes to specialized training programs. Some even offer courses tailored specifically to project managers.

2. Online Resources: The internet is a treasure trove of information, with countless tutorials, webinars, and online courses available to help project managers get up to speed on the latest in AI.

3. Industry Events: Conferences, workshops, and seminars provide opportunities to learn from experts in the field and to network with peers who are also navigating the challenges of integrating AI into project management.

4. In-House Training: Organizations increasingly recognize the importance of upskilling their staff to leverage new technologies. In-house training sessions can be an effective way to disseminate the latest knowledge and best practices across a project management team.

5. Peer-to-Peer Learning: Sometimes the best insights come from those who are in the trenches, dealing with the same challenges. Regularly engaging with other project managers, whether within the same organization or in different industries, can provide valuable perspectives and practical tips for using AI in project management.

6. Professional Journals and Publications: Academic and industry journals often publish articles on the latest research and case studies related to AI in project management. These can provide in-depth insights into what's on the cutting edge.

7. Consult with Experts: Sometimes it's worth bringing in an external consultant with specialized knowledge in AI to provide targeted training or advice.

The integration of AI into project management is a dynamic and rapidly evolving field. To navigate it successfully, project managers must commit to a path of continuous learning, staying abreast of the latest technological advancements, methodologies, and ethical and legal considerations. This investment in ongoing education is not just a means to keep up with the pace of change; it's a critical factor in leveraging the full potential of AI to improve project outcomes.

Ethical Leadership

The integration of Artificial Intelligence (AI) into project management is no longer a futuristic concept but a present-day reality. As AI technologies become more sophisticated and their applications more varied, project managers find themselves at the intersection of technological innovation and ethical responsibility. The ethical and responsible use of AI in projects is not just a matter of compliance or risk mitigation; it's a fundamental duty that project managers must uphold to maintain the integrity of their profession and the well-being of society at large.

Understanding the ethical implications of AI is the first step in this journey. Project managers need to be aware of the potential for AI to perpetuate or even exacerbate existing societal biases. For example, an AI algorithm trained on biased historical data could make hiring recommendations that are discriminatory. Therefore, project managers must work closely with data scientists and AI experts to ensure that the data sets used to train algorithms are as unbiased and representative as possible. This might involve a thorough audit of the data and even the sourcing of new, more inclusive data sets.

Transparency is another critical ethical consideration. AI algorithms, particularly those based on complex machine learning models, can be opaque, making it difficult to understand how they arrive at specific decisions or recommendations. This "black box" nature of AI can be problematic in many project settings, especially when the stakes are high, as in healthcare or public services projects. Project managers must advocate for the use of explainable AI models or, at the very least, ensure that there is a mechanism for auditing the algorithm's decisions post-hoc.

Data privacy is another area where ethical responsibility comes into play. AI algorithms often require access to large amounts of data, some of which may be sensitive or personal. Project managers must ensure that all data used in an AI project is handled responsibly, in compliance with data protection laws such as the General Data Protection Regulation (GDPR) in Europe or the California Consumer Privacy Act (CCPA) in the United States. This involves not just secure storage and handling of data, but also obtaining informed consent from individuals whose data is being used.

Accountability is also a significant concern. When an AI system makes a decision, who is responsible if something goes wrong? Is it the project manager, the data scientist, the end-user, or the organization as a whole? Clear lines of accountability must be established before the project begins, and these should be communicated to all stakeholders. This might also involve creating a framework for redress for those adversely affected by decisions made by the AI system.

Finally, the ethical responsibility of a project manager extends to the long-term impact of the AI system. It's not enough to consider only the immediate outcomes of implementing AI; project managers must also think about the sustainability and long-term ethical implications. For example, if the AI system is designed to automate certain jobs, what plans are in place to retrain or support the workers who will be displaced?

The ethical and responsible implementation of AI in projects is a complex but crucial aspect of modern project management. It requires a multi-faceted approach that considers not just the technological capabilities of AI, but also its broader societal, ethical, and human implications. Project managers, therefore, have a significant role to play in shaping the ethical landscape of AI, a responsibility that should be embraced as both a professional duty and a moral imperative.

Collaboration and Networking

The interdisciplinary nature of Artificial Intelligence (AI) presents both a challenge and an opportunity for project managers. As AI technologies become increasingly integrated into various aspects of project management, from data analytics and decision-making to resource allocation and stakeholder engagement, the complexity of managing these projects also rises. This complexity is not just technical but also ethical, legal, and social. Therefore, project managers stand to gain immensely from collaborating with experts in various domains, including data science, machine learning, and ethics.

Collaboration with data scientists is particularly crucial for the effective implementation of AI in projects. Data scientists bring a deep understanding of data structures, statistical methods, and machine learning algorithms. They can help project managers make sense of the vast amounts of data that AI algorithms need for training and operation. More importantly, data scientists can guide project managers in selecting the most appropriate algorithms for their specific project goals, whether it's predictive analytics for risk assessment or natural language processing for customer engagement. This collaborative relationship allows for a more nuanced approach to problem-solving, one that combines the project manager's understanding of objectives and constraints with the data scientist's technical expertise.

Machine learning experts, on the other hand, can provide valuable insights into the design, training, and validation of complex AI models. They can help project managers understand the limitations and assumptions behind different machine learning techniques, from simple linear regression models to complex neural networks. This understanding is crucial for setting realistic project goals, timelines, and budgets. Machine learning experts can also assist in the iterative process of model training and refinement, ensuring that the AI system meets the project's performance criteria while adhering to ethical guidelines for fairness and transparency.

Ethics experts play a vital role in ensuring that AI projects are conducted responsibly. They can help project managers navigate the complex ethical landscape that surrounds AI, from issues of data privacy and consent to algorithmic fairness and accountability. Ethics experts can provide a framework for ethical decision-making, helping project managers identify potential ethical pitfalls and develop strategies to mitigate them. They can also facilitate stakeholder engagement on ethical issues, ensuring that the project's ethical considerations are transparent and aligned with broader societal values.

In essence, the integration of AI into project management is not merely a technical endeavor but a deeply interdisciplinary one. It requires a collaborative approach that draws on expertise from various domains. Project managers, by actively seeking out and collaborating with experts in data science, machine learning, and ethics, can ensure that their AI projects are not only technically sound but also ethically responsible and socially beneficial. This interdisciplinary collaboration enriches the project management process, leading to more innovative, effective, and ethical outcomes.

Section 3: Future Trends to Watch

AI and Augmented Reality (AR)

The fusion of Artificial Intelligence (AI) with Augmented Reality (AR) is a technological marriage that promises to redefine the boundaries of what's possible in various domains, particularly in areas like training and real-time data visualization. While AI brings the power of data analytics, machine learning, and natural language processing, AR contributes the ability to overlay digital information onto the physical world. Together, they offer a transformative set of tools that can make training more interactive, data visualization more intuitive, and real-time decision-making more informed.

In the context of training, the integration of AI with AR can create highly personalized, interactive, and context-aware experiences. Imagine a medical training program where a surgeon, wearing AR glasses, performs a complex procedure. The AI system could analyze the surgeon's movements in real-time, offering instant feedback and guidance through the AR display. If the surgeon reaches a critical step, the AI could overlay relevant data or diagrams directly onto the surgical field, enhancing the surgeon's understanding and reducing the likelihood of errors. The system could even simulate potential complications, allowing the surgeon to practice responses in a safe but realistic environment. This level of personalized, context-aware training could dramatically improve the effectiveness of educational programs across various fields, from healthcare and engineering to military and emergency response.

When it comes to real-time data visualization, the synergy between AI and AR is equally compelling. In a manufacturing setting, for instance, a maintenance engineer wearing AR glasses could walk through a facility and see machine performance data superimposed on the actual machines. The AI system could analyze this data in real-time to identify potential issues before they become critical failures, flagging them on the engineer's AR display. The system could even suggest preventive actions, overlaying step-by-step repair instructions onto the engineer's field of view. This real-time, context-aware data visualization could significantly improve operational efficiency, reduce downtime, and enhance safety.

Moreover, the AI algorithms can be trained to recognize patterns or anomalies that might be too subtle for a human to detect quickly. For example, in a logistics hub, an AR system could highlight packages that are out of place, mislabeled, or showing signs of damage, allowing for immediate corrective action. The AI could also predict bottlenecks in the sorting process before they occur, enabling preemptive reorganization. This kind of predictive, real-time data visualization could be a game-changer in complex operations where timing and accuracy are critical.

However, the integration of AI and AR is not without challenges. There are issues related to data privacy, especially when sensitive information is displayed in a shared physical space. There are also technical challenges related to the seamless integration of AI analytics and AR visualization, requiring robust, low-latency communication between the two systems. Furthermore, the design of intuitive, user-friendly interfaces is crucial for the effective use of these advanced technologies, necessitating a deep understanding of human factors and ergonomics.

The integration of AI with AR has the potential to revolutionize training and real-time data visualization, among other applications. By combining AI's analytical prowess with AR's intuitive display capabilities, this technological synergy can create more effective, efficient, and engaging experiences. As these technologies continue to mature, their integrated applications could redefine best practices and set new standards for excellence in various fields.

AI in Sustainable Project Management

As the world grapples with the escalating challenges of climate change, resource depletion, and social inequality, the concept of sustainability has moved from the periphery to the core of global discourse. In this context, Artificial Intelligence (AI) emerges not merely as a technological innovation but as a transformative tool that can drive sustainability in various sectors, including project management. By optimizing projects for environmental and social sustainability, AI can contribute to a more responsible and resilient future.

In the realm of environmental sustainability, AI can provide project managers with the tools to make more informed decisions that reduce the environmental impact of their projects. For instance, AI algorithms can analyze vast amounts of data to predict the environmental consequences of different project strategies. In a construction project, AI could assess the carbon footprint of various building materials, the energy efficiency of different construction methods, and even the long-term environmental impact of a building's design. This kind of predictive analysis can guide project managers in selecting the most sustainable options, from the planning phase right through to execution and beyond.

AI can also help in real-time monitoring of environmental factors. For example, in an industrial setting, AI-powered sensors could continuously monitor emissions, waste production, and energy usage. If any of these metrics approach unsustainable levels, the AI system could alert project managers immediately, enabling timely interventions. In some cases, the AI could even be programmed to make automatic adjustments to machinery or systems to reduce environmental impact, without human intervention. This real-time responsiveness can be invaluable in minimizing the environmental footprint of industrial projects.

When it comes to social sustainability, AI has the potential to make significant contributions as well. One of the key aspects of social sustainability is inclusivity, ensuring that projects do not marginalize or adversely affect certain groups of people. AI algorithms can analyze demographic data, local laws, and community sentiments to help project managers understand the social implications of their decisions. For instance, if a proposed infrastructure project threatens to displace a vulnerable community, AI can help identify alternative solutions that are less disruptive. Moreover, AI can assist in stakeholder engagement by analyzing public sentiments expressed on social media or through community surveys, providing project managers with insights into the concerns and expectations of the communities involved.

AI can also contribute to the economic aspects of social sustainability by optimizing for cost-efficiency in a way that benefits not just the organization but also the broader community. For example, in public transport projects, AI can optimize routes and schedules to serve the maximum number of people at the lowest cost, making public transport more accessible and reducing the community's overall carbon footprint.

However, the application of AI in sustainability is not without its challenges. One of the primary concerns is the ethical use of data, especially when analyzing sensitive environmental or demographic information. Project managers must adhere to strict data privacy laws and ethical guidelines to ensure that the data used for sustainability optimization is handled responsibly. Additionally, there's the challenge of 'greenwashing,' where the purported sustainability benefits of a project are exaggerated or falsely claimed. AI systems must be designed and used transparently to avoid such pitfalls.

As the urgency for sustainability intensifies, AI offers a powerful set of tools for project managers to optimize for both environmental and social sustainability. From predictive analytics and real-time monitoring to stakeholder engagement and ethical considerations, AI can play a multifaceted role in driving sustainable practices in project management. While challenges exist, the potential benefits of integrating AI into sustainable project management are too significant to ignore. As AI technologies continue to evolve, their role in facilitating a more sustainable future is likely to grow, offering new avenues for innovation and responsibility in project management.

The Democratization of AI

The democratization of Artificial Intelligence (AI) is a transformative trend that is leveling the playing field in various industries, including project management. Gone are the days when the use of AI was restricted to large corporations with deep pockets and specialized teams of data scientists. Today, the increasing user-friendliness and accessibility of AI tools are enabling smaller organizations and even individual project managers to leverage these advanced technologies for more effective and efficient project outcomes.

One of the most significant shifts we are witnessing is the development of AI platforms that are designed with the end-user in mind. These platforms often come with intuitive interfaces, easy-to-understand dashboards, and step-by-step guides that make it easier for individuals who may not have a background in data science to navigate the complexities of AI algorithms. This user-centric design approach is making it possible for project managers to set up and run AI-powered analyses without requiring specialized training or expertise.

Moreover, the rise of cloud computing has made it easier for smaller organizations to access powerful AI algorithms without the need for expensive hardware or software installations. Cloud-based AI services offer scalable solutions that can be customized to fit the specific needs and budgets of smaller projects. This flexibility allows project managers to experiment with AI functionalities at a lower risk and cost, providing them with the opportunity to understand the value that AI can bring to their projects before committing to larger-scale implementations.

The availability of pre-trained models and templates is another factor contributing to the accessibility of AI for smaller organizations and individual project managers. These ready-made solutions can be adapted to suit specific project needs, saving time and resources that would otherwise be spent on developing algorithms from scratch. For example, a project manager in a small construction firm could use a pre-trained machine learning model to predict potential delays and cost overruns based on historical data and current project conditions.

AI's growing accessibility is also being fueled by a burgeoning ecosystem of third-party developers and vendors who offer specialized AI tools tailored for various aspects of project management. Whether it's risk assessment, resource allocation, or stakeholder engagement, there is likely an AI tool available that is designed to address that specific challenge. These specialized tools often come with the added benefit of community support, tutorials, and case studies that guide project managers in implementing AI in the most effective manner.

However, the increasing accessibility of AI tools does not eliminate the need for a strategic approach to their implementation. Project managers, regardless of the size of their organization, must still exercise due diligence in selecting the right tools that align with their project objectives. They must also be mindful of ethical considerations such as data privacy and algorithmic bias, which are as relevant in smaller-scale projects as they are in large enterprises.

The growing user-friendliness and accessibility of AI tools are opening up new possibilities for smaller organizations and individual project managers. From cloud-based solutions and pre-trained models to a wide array of specialized tools, AI is becoming increasingly integrated into the fabric of project management at all levels. While challenges and considerations remain, the democratization of AI holds the promise of more equitable access to advanced technologies, thereby empowering a broader range of project managers to drive innovation, efficiency, and success.

Section 4: Challenges and Risks Ahead

Data Security

The integration of Artificial Intelligence (AI) into project management is a double-edged sword. On one hand, it offers unprecedented capabilities for data analysis, resource allocation, and decision-making. On the other hand, the very features that make AI so valuable also make it an attractive target for cyberattacks. As AI systems become more deeply embedded in the operations and decision-making processes of projects, the potential impact of a successful cyberattack grows exponentially, raising the stakes for project managers to ensure robust cybersecurity measures are in place.

The vulnerabilities associated with AI systems in project management are manifold. For instance, machine learning algorithms often require access to large datasets, which may include sensitive or proprietary information. If a cyberattacker were to gain unauthorized access to these datasets, the consequences could range from data theft and corporate espionage to severe financial and reputational damage. Moreover, AI algorithms themselves could be the target of attacks aimed at altering their functionality. Such attacks could subtly change the behavior of the algorithm in a way that might not be immediately noticeable but could have significant long-term consequences, such as making poor resource allocation decisions or failing to identify project risks.

Another area of concern is the potential for 'adversarial attacks,' which are designed to deceive machine learning models by feeding them misleading data. In the context of project management, an adversarial attack could, for example, manipulate the AI system into underestimating the time or resources required for a project, leading to overcommitment and eventual project failure. These types of attacks are particularly insidious because they exploit the very logic that the AI system uses to make decisions, making them difficult to detect without rigorous monitoring and validation processes.

The increasing use of cloud-based AI solutions adds another layer of complexity to the cybersecurity landscape. While cloud platforms often provide scalable and cost-effective solutions for implementing AI in project management, they also introduce additional points of vulnerability. These platforms can be susceptible to a range of cyber threats, including data breaches and denial-of-service attacks, which could disrupt access to critical project management tools and data.

Given these risks, project managers must adopt a proactive approach to cybersecurity. This involves not just implementing state-of-the-art security protocols but also continuously monitoring and updating these measures to adapt to evolving threats. Cybersecurity is no longer just the domain of IT specialists; it's a critical competency that project managers must develop to protect the integrity of their projects in an AI-driven environment.

Regular audits and stress tests of the AI system can help identify vulnerabilities before they can be exploited. Additionally, project managers should work closely with cybersecurity experts to develop incident response plans specifically tailored to the types of AI being used in the project. These plans should outline the steps to be taken in the event of a cyberattack, including how to isolate affected systems, communicate with stakeholders, and recover lost data or functionality.

The integration of AI into project management offers exciting possibilities for efficiency and innovation but also presents new challenges in the form of increased cybersecurity risks. As AI systems become more central to the functioning of projects, the potential impact of cyberattacks on these systems grows, making it imperative for project managers to prioritize cybersecurity measures that are as sophisticated and adaptive as the AI systems they aim to protect.

Regulatory Changes

The rapid advancement of Artificial Intelligence (AI) is prompting governments worldwide to grapple with its far-reaching implications. As AI becomes more integrated into various sectors, including project management, governments are increasingly recognizing the need for comprehensive regulations to ensure responsible and ethical AI use. These emerging regulations have the potential to significantly impact how AI is implemented in projects across different industries.

1. Data Privacy and Security Regulations: Many governments have already implemented or are considering strict data privacy and security regulations, such as the European Union's General Data Protection Regulation (GDPR) and the California Consumer Privacy Act (CCPA). These regulations impose stringent requirements on how organizations handle and protect personal data. In project management, where AI often relies on vast datasets, compliance with these regulations is crucial. Project managers must ensure that AI systems handle data in a privacy-compliant manner, which can involve data anonymization, secure storage, and user consent mechanisms.
2. Algorithmic Fairness and Transparency: Governments are increasingly concerned about algorithmic bias and discrimination, especially when AI systems are used in critical decision-making processes, such as hiring or lending. To address this, regulations may require transparency in AI algorithms and mechanisms to detect and mitigate bias. Project managers implementing AI in projects will need to ensure that their systems comply with these fairness and transparency standards, including conducting bias audits and providing explanations for AI-driven decisions.
3. Ethical Frameworks and Guidelines: Some governments are developing ethical frameworks and guidelines for AI, outlining principles and best practices for responsible AI use. These frameworks often emphasize human-centric AI, accountability, and the prevention of harm. Project managers may be required to align their AI implementations with these ethical guidelines, promoting the responsible use of AI in project decision-making and operations.
4. Liability and Accountability: Questions surrounding liability for AI-related errors and accidents are being addressed by governments. Regulations may establish liability frameworks for AI systems, specifying who is responsible in case of AI-related harm or failure. Project managers

147

must consider these liability provisions when implementing AI, as they may affect project contracts, insurance, and risk management strategies.

5. Certification and Accreditation: Some governments are exploring certification and accreditation programs for AI systems. These programs aim to ensure the quality and safety of AI applications. Project managers may need to seek certification for AI components used in their projects, ensuring compliance with government standards.

6. International Collaboration: AI is a global phenomenon, and governments recognize the importance of international collaboration on AI regulation. Efforts like the OECD's AI Principles and agreements on cross-border data flow are emerging. Project managers involved in international projects should be aware of these collaborations and consider their impact on AI implementation and data management across borders.

7. Research and Development Funding: Governments are also playing a role in advancing AI through research and development funding. They are investing in AI projects with potential societal benefits, such as healthcare, transportation, and infrastructure. Project managers may find opportunities for collaboration and funding in these government-led initiatives.

In conclusion, as governments worldwide grapple with the implications of AI, project managers must stay informed about evolving regulations that could impact AI implementation in their projects. Being proactive in understanding and complying with these regulations is essential for responsible and ethical AI integration into project management practices. Additionally, project managers can contribute to the development of best practices and standards that align with emerging regulatory frameworks, ensuring that AI enhances project outcomes while maintaining ethical and legal integrity.

Social and Cultural Resistance

The fear of job displacement and a general mistrust of AI represent substantial challenges to the widespread adoption of this transformative technology. While AI offers numerous benefits, including increased efficiency and productivity, it also raises concerns about its impact on employment and job security. Addressing these concerns and building trust in AI are essential steps for fostering its successful integration into various industries, including project management.

1. Reskilling and Upskilling: One way to mitigate the fear of job displacement is through reskilling and upskilling programs. Project managers, alongside organizations, can invest in training employees to work alongside AI systems effectively. These programs can focus on developing skills that complement AI, such as data analysis, problem-solving, and human-AI collaboration. By empowering employees to adapt to the changing landscape, organizations can alleviate concerns about job loss.

2. Job Redefinition: Project managers can emphasize that AI is not necessarily a replacement for human workers but a tool that can augment their capabilities. AI can handle repetitive and mundane tasks, allowing humans to focus on more strategic and creative aspects of their roles.

By redefining job roles to emphasize human-AI collaboration, project managers can ease concerns about job displacement.

3. Transparency and Accountability: Building trust in AI systems requires transparency and accountability in their design and operation. Project managers should ensure that AI algorithms are explainable and that decisions made by AI can be understood by humans. Transparency also involves clearly defining the roles of AI and human workers within a project, setting expectations for how AI will be used, and ensuring that AI is used ethically and responsibly.

4. Ethical Considerations: Addressing ethical concerns related to AI is vital. Project managers must prioritize ethical decision-making and ensure that AI systems do not perpetuate biases or discriminate against certain groups. Implementing robust ethical guidelines and conducting regular audits of AI systems can demonstrate a commitment to responsible AI use.

5. Education and Communication: Effective communication is crucial for overcoming mistrust. Project managers should communicate the benefits of AI adoption clearly and provide educational resources to stakeholders. Sharing success stories and case studies that demonstrate AI's positive impact on projects can help build confidence in the technology.

6. Collaboration with Stakeholders: Involving employees, clients, and other stakeholders in AI adoption processes can help address concerns and gain their support. Engaging stakeholders in discussions about the role of AI, its limitations, and its potential benefits can foster a sense of ownership and participation in AI initiatives.

7. Regulatory Compliance: Staying informed about and complying with relevant labor laws and regulations is essential. Project managers should ensure that AI implementations adhere to legal requirements related to employment, including fair labor practices and anti-discrimination laws.

8. Demonstrating ROI: Project managers should track and communicate the return on investment (ROI) of AI implementations. Demonstrating tangible benefits, such as cost savings, increased efficiency, and improved project outcomes, can help alleviate fears of AI's negative impact on projects and jobs.

While concerns about job displacement and mistrust of AI are valid, project managers can play a pivotal role in addressing these challenges. By fostering a culture of responsible AI adoption, promoting transparency, and emphasizing human-AI collaboration, project managers can pave the way for AI's successful integration into project management practices, ultimately benefiting both organizations and their workforce.

Section 5: Final Recommendations

Stay Informed

Continuously enhancing one's knowledge and staying up-to-date in the fields of AI and project management is crucial for success in an ever-evolving landscape. Here's a detailed approach to accomplishing this through regular reading of publications, conference attendance, and engagement with thought leaders:

Regular Reading of Publications:

1. Identify Trustworthy Sources: To begin, individuals should identify credible and reputable publications that focus on AI developments and project management best practices. These sources can include established journals, industry-specific magazines, and online platforms dedicated to AI advancements and project management.

2. Industry-Specific Publications: Depending on their industry or sector, individuals should subscribe to publications that cater to their specific interests. For instance, someone working in healthcare might choose to follow journals like "Healthcare IT News," while a technology-focused professional may opt for publications like "MIT Technology Review."

3. Academic Journals: Academic journals often publish cutting-edge research in AI and its various applications across industries. Project managers can explore journals such as "Journal of Artificial Intelligence Research" and "Harvard Business Review" to access valuable insights and scholarly work.

Conference Attendance:

1. Identify Relevant Conferences: Individuals should proactively seek out conferences, seminars, and webinars that are related to AI and project management. Events like the Project Management Institute (PMI) Global Conference, AI Summit, and industry-specific conferences provide invaluable opportunities for knowledge sharing and learning.

2. Networking Opportunities: Conferences not only offer access to expert speakers but also provide ample networking opportunities. Attendees can connect with peers, industry professionals, and AI experts, facilitating the exchange of ideas and real-world experiences.

3. Stay Informed About Trends: Conferences often feature sessions on the latest AI trends, case studies, and emerging technologies. Participation in these sessions can offer firsthand insights into how AI is shaping the landscape of project management.

Engagement with Thought Leaders:

1. Identify and Follow Thought Leaders: It's essential to identify and follow thought leaders and experts in the fields of AI and project management. These thought leaders can include authors of influential books, professors, industry leaders, and renowned figures in AI research.

2. Utilize Social Media: Platforms like LinkedIn and Twitter provide excellent avenues for staying connected with thought leaders and participating in meaningful discussions. Joining relevant groups, following experts, and engaging in conversations can contribute significantly to staying well-informed.

3. Leverage Online Forums: Active participation in online forums and communities dedicated to AI and project management can be an excellent source of knowledge. These platforms allow individuals to ask questions, share insights, and learn from others' experiences.

4. Explore Blogs and Podcasts: Many thought leaders maintain blogs or host podcasts where they share their expertise and discuss industry trends. Subscribing to these resources can provide a steady stream of valuable information and insights.

Knowledge Sharing:

1. Promote Internal Knowledge Sharing: Within their organizations, individuals should actively encourage knowledge sharing among team members. Organizing knowledge-sharing sessions or discussions where team members can exchange information and share their experiences related to AI implementations can be highly beneficial.
2. Mentorship: Establishing mentoring relationships with AI experts or seasoned project managers can provide invaluable guidance and insights. Mentors can offer practical advice and help individuals navigate the complexities of AI and project management effectively.

Staying informed and continuously expanding one's knowledge base in AI and project management is an ongoing commitment that yields substantial benefits. Regularly reading reputable publications, actively participating in conferences, and engaging with thought leaders are key pillars of this journey toward expertise and excellence in these dynamic fields.

Be Proactive, Not Reactive

Proactive exploration and integration of AI into project management can yield significant advantages, so waiting for it to become a necessity is not advisable. Here's a detailed breakdown of why you should start exploring AI's benefits for your projects right away:

1. Competitive Advantage: Early adopters of AI in project management gain a competitive edge. By embracing AI technologies ahead of the curve, you position yourself and your organization as innovators in your industry. This can lead to increased market share and business growth.
2. Efficiency Improvements: AI can automate routine tasks, optimize resource allocation, and provide real-time insights, significantly increasing project efficiency. By adopting AI early, you can realize efficiency improvements that may not be attainable through traditional methods.
3. Cost Savings: AI-driven automation can lead to substantial cost savings over time. Reduced labor costs, minimized errors, and better resource utilization can all contribute to a healthier bottom line for your projects.
4. Risk Mitigation: AI can analyze historical data to predict risks and provide early warnings. By implementing AI tools from the outset, you can proactively identify and address potential project risks, ensuring smoother project execution.
5. Improved Decision-Making: AI algorithms can process and analyze vast datasets, providing project managers with data-driven insights for decision-making. Starting early allows you to make more informed and strategic decisions throughout the project lifecycle.

151

6. Enhanced Stakeholder Satisfaction: AI can improve communication, stakeholder engagement, and project transparency. Engaging with AI solutions early can lead to better stakeholder relationships and increased satisfaction with project outcomes.

7. Learning Curve: Integrating AI into project management involves a learning curve. By starting early, you can gradually build your expertise and experience with AI tools, ensuring that you and your team are well-prepared to maximize their potential.

8. Innovation Culture: Early exploration of AI fosters an innovative culture within your organization. It encourages a mindset of continuous improvement and an openness to adopting emerging technologies, which can benefit all aspects of your projects.

9. Adaptability: As your projects evolve, you may encounter new challenges or requirements that AI can address. By already having some familiarity with AI solutions, you can adapt more swiftly to changing project needs.

10. Future-Proofing: The world of project management is evolving, and AI is becoming increasingly integral. By embracing AI early, you future-proof your skills and your organization, ensuring relevance and competitiveness in the years to come.

11. Networking and Collaboration: Engaging with AI at an early stage allows you to network and collaborate with AI experts and solution providers. Building these relationships can lead to valuable partnerships and access to cutting-edge technologies.

12. Experimentation: Starting early gives you the freedom to experiment with different AI tools and approaches. You can assess which solutions align best with your project management style and objectives without the pressure of immediate necessity.

Beginning your exploration of AI's potential benefits for project management now offers numerous advantages. It not only positions you as an industry leader but also equips you with the tools and knowledge to drive efficiency, reduce costs, and make data-driven decisions that can positively impact your projects. Early adoption of AI is a strategic move that can pave the way for long-term success in project management.

Conclusion: The Journey Has Just Begun

The integration of AI into project management is a journey, not a destination. It's a dynamic field, with new advancements and challenges emerging regularly. By staying informed, adaptable, and ethically responsible, project managers can navigate this transformative landscape successfully.